THE CORK
SCHOOL OF MEDICINE

A HISTORY

THE CORK
SCHOOL OF MEDICINE

A HISTORY

DENIS J. O'SULLIVAN

UCC
Coláiste na hOllscoile Corcaigh, Éire
University College Cork, Ireland

First published in 2007 by the
UCC Medical Alumni Association
University College Cork,
Ireland

© 2007, Denis J. O'Sullivan

British Library Cataloguing in Publication Data

A CIP catalogue record for this book is available from the British Library.

ISBN-13: 978 0 9552229 4 8
ISBN-10: 0 9552229 4 X

Designed and Typeset by Anú Design, Tara (www.anu-design.ie)

Printed in Ireland by Colourbooks

Contents

Illustrations

Front Cover:
Flame, by Alexandra Wejchert (1920–1995)
This remarkable sculpture in brass on a granite plinth is situated in the Department of Anatomy, UCC. It signifies the altruism of all who donate their bodies for medical science and education. It represents the 'Flame of Knowledge which leads to the Light of Understanding' (P.B. Medawar) and was commissioned as part of the commemoration of the 150th anniversary of the founding of University College Cork in 1995 (UCC Collection, Andrew Bradley Photography)

Back Cover:
Benches in the Anatomy Lecture Theatre, Windle Building, UCC (UCC Collection, Andrew Bradley Photography)

Page xi   The Windle Building, 2007, UCC (UCC Collection, Andrew Bradley Photography)

Page 2   Queen Victoria's carriage on Western Road passing the newly completed Queen's College, August 1849 (Copy of an original engraving by Scraggs, University Archives, UCC, UC\PH\2)

Page 3   The opening of Queen's College Cork (QCC), 7 November 1849 (*Illustrated London News).*

Page 5   Sir Robert Kane, first President, QCC, 1845–1871 (University Archives, UCC, UC\PH\PD\2)

Page 9   Alcock's Canal, coronal sections through the *Canalis Pudendalis* (courtesy of Ronan O'Rahilly, *A History of the Cork Medical School: 1849–1949,* p. 34)

            Benjamin Alcock, first Professor of Anatomy and Physiology, QCC, 1849–1854 (Private Collection)

Foreword

I have been associated with University College Cork for more than fifty years. In all of this time, the Medical School has been my main interest. For much of it, I was chiefly concerned with current events, with the recent past and the immediate future. Over the years, however, the overall story of the school has increasingly interested me, and, in later years, I have made a number of presentations and have written some papers about its history. Because of this, a few of my colleagues urged me to write a history of the Medical School. They felt that there was a need for this, given that the faculty is over 150 years old and the last account of it was written more than fifty years ago. I was slow to accede to their requests, as I am not a historian and was disinclined to commit myself to a definitive work because of a mixture of ignorance, modesty and sloth. With the passing of the years, however, I began to feel that I owed it to the school to record some of my knowledge and experience of it and that even an incomplete and imperfect work was better than none at all. It was with these rather negative sentiments that I set about writing this story which I have entitled a 'history' with some embarrassment, and for want of a more modest and correct description.

In spite of my reservations, I have enjoyed the task – perhaps more than readers will the end product – because it has resulted in many contacts with friends and former colleagues who have been immensely helpful. To single out a few is, I know, invidious, but doctors Michael Hyland and Paule Cotter, and Professor Barry Ferriss were especially helpful with their advice, script reading and suggestions. Professors John Fraher, John W. Hall, Cuimín Doyle and Eamonn Quigley, together with doctors Anne Gaffney, Margaret O'Connor, Michael Bennett, Raymond Fielding and Peter Kearney contributed in a variety of ways to make this volume possible. The staff at the medical faculty office and the Health Service Executive, the Cork Farm Centre and the individual hospitals were unfailing in their willingness to supply information. Ms Evelyn Murray of the Health Services Executive was particularly helpful in providing information regarding Our Lady's Hospital. Professor Michael B. Murphy, Dean of Medicine and Health, and Head of the College of Medicine and Health, contributed in many ways and deserves my special gratitude, as do Ms Rita Lynch and Ms Catherine Roantree, who, with their skills in typing, computing and editing, made up for my woeful deficiencies in all of these regards. Virginia Teehan, former University College Cork archivist, freely facilitated access to records relating to student numbers. Nancy Hawkes of UCC's Office of Marketing and Communications was patient, kind and very helpful in editing the book for publication.

Finally, I want to thank my wife, Joan, without whose constant help and encouragement none of this would have been possible.

The Windle Building, UCC

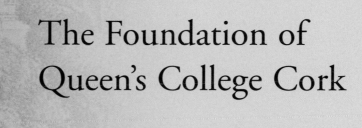

1

The Foundation of Queen's College Cork

Queen's College Cork was formally opened on 7 November 1849. This was consequent on the powers of the Colleges of Ireland Act of 1845 which decreed the establishment of the Queen's University in Ireland and its three constituent colleges: Belfast, Cork and Galway. Queen's College Cork came into existence formally on 30 December 1845 by a charter of incorporation which ordained that there be three faculties: Arts, Law and Physic. The charter named Sir Robert Kane as president and John Ryall as vice-president. It was planned that the college would be non-sectarian, non-residential and low-fee, with systemic lecturing rather than a tutorial system, such as prevailed at Oxford and Cambridge.

Building commenced in 1847 and was completed in 1849. The architect was Sir Thomas Deane, a leading Cork architect whose firm designed a number of the city's most important buildings of the time, including the Cork Savings Bank and St Mary's Church, Pope's Quay. Deane is known to have borrowed a collection of drawings of Oxford colleges from a colleague and it is said that his plan of the college was influenced by Magdalen College in particular.[1] He presented a statue of Queen Victoria (executed by Edward Ambrose, the Cork sculptor) to the college authorities in 1849 for erection in the most conspicuous position in the college tower. The young queen herself paid a brief visit to Cork in August 1849 and although she did not visit the near-completed building site, she drove along the Western Road in her carriage from where she could view the college. As she passed, all work was suspended and the statue was erected suddenly in her full view. To add to the occasion, the Royal Standard could be seen waving in the air, and, under it, those of the various trades employed in the work. The statue was to play its part in college history later (see p. 107).

The formal opening, on 7 November 1849, was a splendid affair. It took place in the Aula Maxima which was tightly packed with college dignitaries, corporation members, representatives of the city's business and intellectual life, and many distinguished visitors.

Queen Victoria's carriage on Western Road passing the newly completed Queen's College Cork, August 1849

The opening of Queen's College Cork, 7 November 1849

The inaugural address was given by the new president, Sir Robert Kane, and took more than two hours. The visitors included Dr Dominic Corrigan, the first Catholic President of the Royal College of Physicians of Ireland.

The medical faculty was opened the following day by the Dean and Professor of Surgery, Dr Denis Bullen. Dr Bullen had played an important part in the considerable efforts, which had taken place for more than a decade prior to the opening, to establish a college in Cork. The arguments in favour of this were multiple and persuasive: prominent among them was the desirability, and indeed the need, for a College Medical School. Cork already had a number of medical schools and, in fact, there was a highly successful one in operation at the time of the college's opening. Thus an adequate supply of students was guaranteed. Among the less attractive but cogent arguments put forward by Bullen was the plenitude of paupers in Cork who would offer ample opportunity for the study of anatomy and certain aspects of pathology.

Other Cork Medical Schools

Prior to the opening of Queen's College and its associated medical school, medicine had been taught in Cork for almost 150 years. There were five medical schools in Cork during this time. The first of these was established in 1722, in association with the South Infirmary, with anatomy taught in a dissecting room on the nearby Old Blackrock

Road. The rest were all established in the early years of the nineteenth century, largely because there was then a great demand for doctors in the British army and navy due to the Napoleonic wars. Three of these – the Dissecting Room in Cove Street, 1812–1828, the School of Anatomy in Warren's (now Parnell) Place, 1828–1835 and the School of Anatomy, Medicine and Surgery (its successor also in Warren's Place), 1835–1844 – were either founded by or closely associated with John Woodroffe, a surgeon at the South Infirmary. According to Coakley,[2] they produced a number of distinguished doctors but were better known for the students of art who studied anatomy under Woodroffe; the surgeon exerted a deep influence on some of the greatest Irish artists of the nineteenth century, including the painter Daniel Maclise and the sculptor John Hogan. Though he was not on the staff of the new medical faculty, he was clearly held in high regard by its members who paid him many tributes.

The Recognised School of Medicine, 1828–1858, a rival institution which continued for at least ten years after Queen's College Cork was established, was situated on the South Mall. It was founded by Henry Augustus Caesar, a somewhat flamboyant character who had been Acting Assistant Surgeon to several regiments and who, in addition to being 'President' and 'Proprietor' was also 'Professor' and 'Lecturer' in Anatomy and Physiology. The school was not over modest, describing itself in *The Medical Directory*[3] as 'midway between the North and South infirmaries … its system of Education is so complete, that gentlemen have become Members of the Royal College of Surgeons, England, 48 hours after leaving Cork'. The classes in practical anatomy included 'an unlimited number of subjects' – a brave statement after the Anatomy Act of 1832 which laid down firm recommendations regarding the availability of subjects for anatomical examination.[4]

The First President, Robert Kane

Robert Kane, Queen's College Cork (QCC's) first president, was a man of extraordinary talent. He was the son of John Kane who, as a young man, had to leave Dublin for Paris because of his involvement with the United Irishmen. There, he studied chemistry and on his return to Dublin, where Robert was born in 1809, he founded a chemical factory. Robert was a brilliant student who, from an early age, was interested in chemistry although he actually studied medicine. This he did at Apothecaries Hall in Dublin where he received his licentiate in 1829. While a student, he published significant papers in both medicine and chemistry and studied at Trinity College Dublin where he took his BA, but not a medical degree. After obtaining his licentiate, he worked at the

Meath Hospital (then the centre of medical science in Dublin), where he was a clinical clerk with William Stokes and Robert Graves, two of Ireland's most famous physicians. He continued to publish and win prizes in medicine and chemistry and in 1831, when he was aged twenty-two, was appointed Professor of Chemistry in the Apothecaries Hall. The following year, he obtained the licentiate of the Irish College of Physicians and was elected a Fellow of the College in 1841.

After leaving the Meath Hospital, Robert ceased practising clinical medicine and became deeply interested in industrial chemistry. By his mid-thirties, he had become a chemist of international repute

Sir Robert Kane, first President, Queen's College Cork, 1845–1871

and among his, by then, many publications in both medicine and chemistry was *The Industrial Resources of Ireland*, which gained him much favour among economically orientated young Irish nationalists. He was also the author of a standard textbook of chemistry in three volumes in 1841–42. He became a Fellow of the Royal Society in 1842 and held high office in many prestigious Dublin societies.

Robert Kane seemed, in many ways, the ideal president of the new college. He was a Catholic to please the majority community which had recently become influential but whose leaders, by and large, disapproved of the new colleges, regarding them as alien and resenting the fact that the clergy had no part in their governing structures; he was also a distinguished scientist with interests in chemistry, industry and medicine. Through his father, he had a whiff of nationalism but he was also clearly held in the highest regard by the Dublin establishment. His appointment to Cork in 1845 was predictably widely acclaimed and was further enhanced by his knighthood the following year. He held the presidency for twenty-eight years until his resignation in 1873, the longest term of office of any president.

Yet his presidency is not viewed as one of unqualified success. He had difficulties with many staff members, starting with Professor Benjamin Alcock in 1853 (see p. 8) but continuing with a succession of others less difficult and held in higher esteem than the troublesome Professor of Anatomy. Many of these disputes were widely publicised and while it is par for the course for a university head to have his troubles with academic colleagues, Kane's were serious and numerous enough to give the overall impression of a troubled presidency in a troubled institution. Added to this was the fact that he was very frequently missing from the college and from Cork. Most of his absences were to his native Dublin where he continued to have considerable involvement in a number of bodies, and indeed the impression that he was 'double-jobbing' was widely held in Cork. This diminished both his efficiency and authority in QCC and he was blamed for 'poor conditions and low morale' in the college. Nowhere was this more vehemently voiced than among the medical students of the time.

Kane resigned the presidency in 1873, citing age (he was sixty-four) and indifferent health (for which he blamed the Cork climate) as the main reasons. He returned to his beloved Dublin (which some of his critics say he never left!), where he enjoyed an active and influential retirement until his death in 1890. Murphy records that he left Cork with a surprisingly good pension.[5] Judgement of his presidency has to be mixed. He successfully established a new college with high educational standards and ideals. His personal prestige was of great help to a struggling, new, provincial institution. He was courageous in defending the principle of a mixed, non-sectarian system from its many detractors. His tenure was undoubtedly clouded, however, by his seeming inability to have good relationships with his staff and his very frequent absences from the college.

2

Cork's First
Medical Faculty

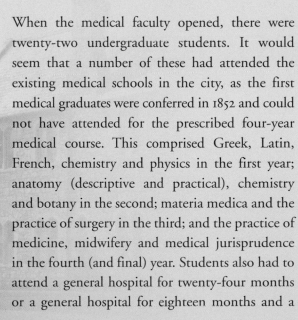

When the medical faculty opened, there were twenty-two undergraduate students. It would seem that a number of these had attended the existing medical schools in the city, as the first medical graduates were conferred in 1852 and could not have attended for the prescribed four-year medical course. This comprised Greek, Latin, French, chemistry and physics in the first year; anatomy (descriptive and practical), chemistry and botany in the second; materia medica and the practice of surgery in the third; and the practice of medicine, midwifery and medical jurisprudence in the fourth (and final) year. Students also had to attend a general hospital for twenty-four months or a general hospital for eighteen months and a dispensary for six months, as well as a course of practical pharmacy for three months. An examination had to be passed in all of the above subjects and the candidate had to be twenty-one years of age before being conferred. The professors appointed to teach the first group of medical students included Benjamin Alcock (anatomy and physiology), John Blyth (chemistry), Alex Fleming (materia medica), Denis Charles O'Connor (medicine), Joshua Reuben Harvey (midwifery) and Denis Brenan Bullen (surgery).

While a number of the staff of the existing Cork medical schools were appointed to the new medical faculty, half of the new professors came from outside Cork. Among the more notable of these was the eponymous Benjamin Alcock, Professor of Anatomy and Physiology.

Benjamin Alcock, his Canal and his Problems

Benjamin Alcock was born in Kilkenny in 1801, the son of a doctor, who was also the second Mayor of Kilkenny, and descended from a long line of doctors. His family were well connected and had lived in Ireland for almost 200 years. He was educated in Dublin and entered Trinity College at the age of eighteen. He studied anatomy from the start and held various teaching posts in Dublin before being appointed Professor of Anatomy at the newly opened school of the Apothecaries Hall in 1837. On his appointment to the chair in Cork, he was succeeded in his Dublin post by Joseph Henry Corbett, who succeeded him again when he left Cork some years later.

Alcock described the canal named after him in *The Cyclopaedia of Anatomy and Physiology*, a work in six volumes published between 1836 and 1839. The description of the canal has apparently been modified somewhat by later workers. While he will be remembered for his anatomical description, his stay in Cork was eventful and turbulent. He had many disputes, most notably with President Kane, but later with a wide variety of people, including the servants of the college (the porters), the dean of the faculty, the Inspector of Anatomy (who happened at the time to be the Professor of Medicine, Denis O'Connor) and the bursar. The reasons for the disputes were multiple and varied. Many concerned the workings of the Anatomy Act but his salary (he was paid £200 per annum, more than the other medical professors but less than the arts professors), his rights to certain fees, his relationship with the students and a variety of other matters were all issues at different times. Dublin Castle described him as 'a perfect pest' and called for his resignation. He did resign in 1854 but, the following year, petitioned Queen Victoria. This was referred to the government in Ireland and resulted in his

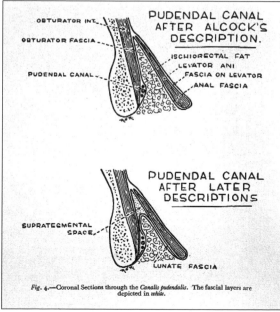

PUDENDAL CANAL
AFTER ALCOCK'S
DESCRIPTION.

OBTURATOR INT.
OBTURATOR FASCIA
PUDENDAL CANAL
ISCHIORECTAL FAT
LEVATOR ANI
FASCIA ON LEVATOR
ANAL FASCIA

PUDENDAL CANAL
AFTER LATER
DESCRIPTIONS

SUPRATEGMENTAL
SPACE
LUNATE FASCIA

Fig. 4.—Coronal Sections through the *Canalis pudendalis*. The fascial layers are depicted in *white*.

ABOVE: *Benjamin Alcock, first Professor of Anatomy and Physiology, Queen's College Cork, 1849–1854.*
LEFT: *Alcock's Canal, coronal sections through the* Canalis Pudendalis, *from Ronan O'Rahilly's* A History of the Cork Medical School: 1849–1949

dismissal in July 1855. According to Cameron's *History*,[1] 'in 1859, being then unmarried, he went to America and has not been since heard of'. As already mentioned, he was replaced by Joseph Henry Corbett, who, in contrast to his turbulent predecessor, had a peaceful incumbency for twenty years.

George Boole

Another of the professors of the new college who was not already in Cork, was the first Professor of Mathematics, George Boole. Although he was not a member of the medical faculty, Boole merits description as he has undoubtedly contributed more to medical science than most medical graduates or teachers. This is because of his contributions to mathematical science; he is widely regarded as the father of modern mathematics and, through his establishment of Boolean algebra, as a very significant figure in the evolution of computer science.

George Boole was born in Lincoln in East Anglia of humble origins. His father was a tradesman and the young George had little or no formal education. Nevertheless, he could read French, Latin and Greek freely when he was sixteen and by the age of twenty had opened a school of his own and had decided that he must learn mathematics thoroughly (which he most certainly did). He had no university degrees on his appointment to Cork and yet was one of its most distinguished professors. As well as his mathematical achievements, he took a full part in academic life: he was an active dean of his faculty, was quite deeply involved in the politics of the young college and had more than one serious disagreement with Kane, the president. Sadly, he died of

George Boole, first Professor of Mathematics, Queen's College Cork, 1849–1864

pneumonia at the comparatively young age of fifty-two. In this regard his wife, Mary Everest (a niece of Sir John Everest, Surveyor-General of India who first surveyed the mountain which bears his name) had, it is said, rather unconventional views on medical treatment and insisted on treating his chest infection by wrapping him in cold, wet garments. George Boole is rightly held in great esteem in UCC, where the main library building bears his name and honours his memory.

The Medical Building

The main quadrangle of Queen's College was completed in 1850. Curiously, no plans appear to have been prepared at this time 'for the more specifically medical lectures nor for the anatomical dissections and demonstrations'.[2] Kane pointed this out rather plaintively in a letter to the Board of Works who were not particularly sympathetic to his complaints and it was left to the generosity of Lord Clarendon, Lord Lieutenant of Ireland at the time, to enable a separate medical building to be built. This was done between 1850 and 1880 at its present site, parallel to the West Wing of the quadrangle. That medicine, which was in the view of many at the time the most important faculty, did not get separate accommodation from the beginning was, as Murphy[3] points out, particularly strange. One of the three wings of the main quadrangle building was

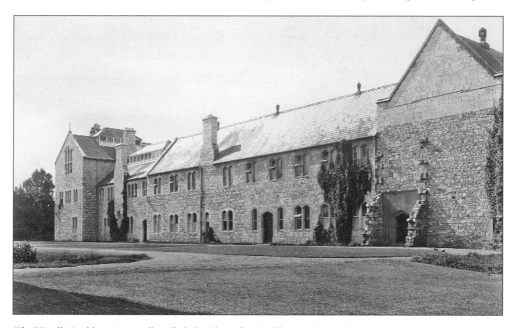

The Windle Building (originally called the Clarendon Building) in the early nineteenth century

allocated as residential space for the president and vice-president. It would appear that then, as so often afterwards, the perceived needs of senior administration took precedence over the real needs of the new college.

The building was named the Clarendon Building after its benefactor. Sullivan, the second president, had plans to extend the building eastwards to connect with the northwest corner of the quadrangle in the hope of providing a spacious library. For a variety of practical reasons, this plan was fortunately shelved; it takes little enough imagination to see what its execution would have done to subsequent mobility and parking arrangements in the college. Sullivan, however, did enlarge the anatomical facilities considerably and later the ground floor was adapted for physiology and, subsequently, for pathology, materia medica and biochemistry. Many of the later enlargements were due to the efforts of Sir Bertram Windle (a later president and himself a pathologist as well as an anatomist and innovator), after whom the building has now been named. In spite of all these efforts, space in the medical building has been pitifully scarce. In 1945, Ronan O'Rahilly wrote hopefully, 'like other medical schools, the Cork College envisages further extensions and new buildings in the future'.[4] He was absolutely correct in his statement, but could hardly have foreseen that these hopes would take half a century to be fulfilled.

The College Fire and the First Dean of Medicine

On the morning of 13 May 1862, Queen's College, then barely a dozen years old, fell victim to a disastrous fire which burned down the entire west wing of the main quadrangle. Fortunately, the other two wings escaped damage but (among others) the departments of chemistry, pathology and materia medica, which were then situated in the wing, were irrevocably damaged, together with a considerable amount of college property and pathological material.

The fire was discovered at 5.45 a.m. and, from the beginning, there was little doubt that it was deliberate and probably executed by someone who had an intimate knowledge of the college and its functions. It was found that efforts had been made to ignite four doors in the cloisters of the wing, and though only one of these had actually caught fire, burned matches were found under all of them. Multiple rumours spread almost immediately, including the colourful, but almost certainly untrue, idea that the fire was connected to a murder case in Waterford where the Clerk of the Union was charged with the murder of his wife by poisoning with arsenic. Specimens from the exhumed woman were being examined by the Professor of Chemistry some hours before the fire.

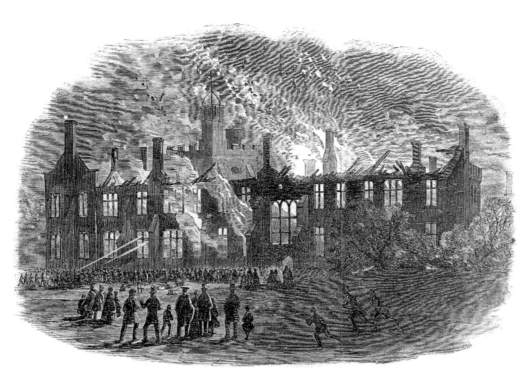

The great college fire, 13 May 1862

Unfortunately, the rumour did not fit the case as the specimens had in fact been examined, the suspect had been charged and the relevant evidence given before the fire had occurred.

Among the many other theories put forward regarding the fire's origin, the most startling and serious was the charge made by one of the professors that the fire was the work of a college official. This was revealed in no less a situation than the House of Commons by an MP, J. Pope Hennessy (a former student of QCC), so it received maximum publicity and clearly required full investigation. The informant was soon revealed and proved to be the Dean of the Medical Faculty and Professor of Surgery, Dr Denis Bullen. He stated that he had strong circumstantial evidence that the fire was the work of a college official and later incriminated the president, Dr Kane himself.

Denis Bullen was an Edinburgh graduate (1823) who was a surgeon at the North Infirmary and lived at 4 Camden Place in Cork (later the home of Mr Edmond Donovan, a distinguished and popular surgeon and lecturer of the mid-twentieth century). He was Inspector of Anatomy for Munster, the author of a number of publications and one of the most active advocates for the establishment of Queen's College and its medical school (citing the need for the latter as one of the strongest arguments for the former).

At the inauguration of the college, he was appointed Professor of Surgery and Dean of the Medical Faculty. He played a prominent role in college affairs from the start and his son was the first student to register at its opening.

With regard to the fire, he stated that the president had suggested to him a few days after the incident, that the two of them should write a report to the government indicating that they considered the fire should be attributed to ultramontane influence. Ultramontanism – the doctrine of supreme papal authority – was widely approved by the Irish Catholic Church at the time and the Church had been at odds with the authorities of Queen's College since the college's establishment. In all, Bullen built up a case strongly suggesting presidential involvement in the fire.

When Bullen's charges were fully investigated, however, they were found to be groundless. When confronted, he admitted to being entirely mistaken, attributed them to a lapse of memory and fully withdrew them. Clearly, the fat was in the fire for Bullen, and it was recommended that he be dismissed. He resigned his chair and was withdrawn from office in 1864.

The reasons for Bullen's extraordinary behaviour have not been fully explained. Kane, as president, had been having multiple difficulties with the college staff and in other regards. It was widely thought in the early 1860s that he would resign the presidency and return to Dublin to take up other distinguished posts. He did little to suggest that this would not happen. It was well known that Bullen was very keen to succeed Kane and this was probably the prime motive for his action. The widespread discontent with Kane in the college and the ongoing controversy about the relationship between the Catholic bishops and the college have also to be taken into account. In the event, neither the exact cause nor the instigators of the fire were ever discovered. Furthermore, Kane continued as president for a further ten years!

At a more general level, the fire was a considerable misfortune for the young medical faculty. Not alone did it cause the loss of its Dean and Professor of Surgery (who was its most influential member), but valuable specimens and instruments were also lost. The Pathological Museum, for example, was destroyed, as was a great deal of property belonging to the materia medica department. As long as fifteen years after the fire, Bullen's successor as dean, Professor D. C. O'Connor, complained bitterly of the great dearth of pathological specimens since the fire. Many requests for recompense for losses sustained fell on the largely deaf ears of the unsympathetic government department of public works.

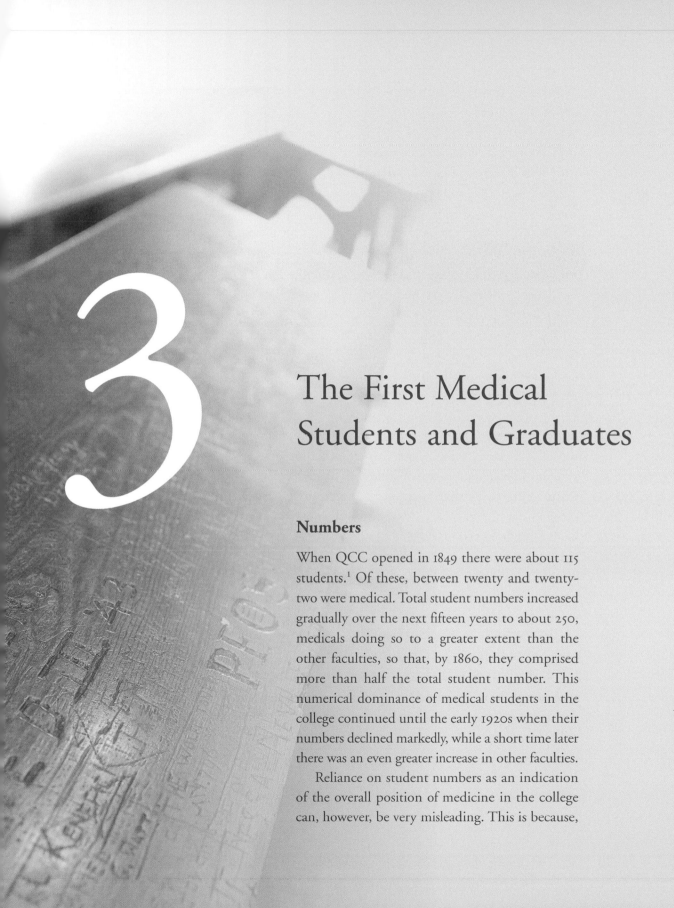

3

The First Medical Students and Graduates

Numbers

When QCC opened in 1849 there were about 115 students.[1] Of these, between twenty and twenty-two were medical. Total student numbers increased gradually over the next fifteen years to about 250, medicals doing so to a greater extent than the other faculties, so that, by 1860, they comprised more than half the total student number. This numerical dominance of medical students in the college continued until the early 1920s when their numbers declined markedly, while a short time later there was an even greater increase in other faculties.

Reliance on student numbers as an indication of the overall position of medicine in the college can, however, be very misleading. This is because,

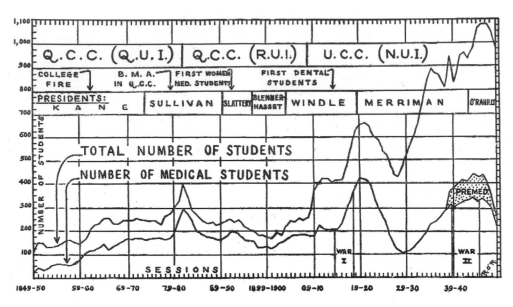

The number of students and medical student numbers at QCC/UCC 1940–1949 from Ronan O'Rahilly's A History of the Cork Medical School: 1849–1949

for most of the nineteenth century, the recorded numbers of students in faculty bore little relationship to the numbers graduating. The reasons for this are multiple and complex. Among the more obvious ones are family and economic circumstances, not infrequent decisions to take up another career, failure in examinations and simple lack of staying power. A more common reason than any of these, however, was that the medical qualification awarded by the Queen's University of Ireland was not held in high standing by some when compared to degrees and diplomas from other examining bodies which could also be taken by QCC students. These latter sometimes gave greater rights of entry to institutions such as the British army. It was possible, for instance, to study at Cork and then travel to London and sit the Membership of the Royal College of Surgeons of that city. The Dublin and Edinburgh Colleges of Surgeons were also favoured. Examinations in these colleges were frequently thought to be easier than those in Queen's University which for Cork students had the added disadvantage of being held in Dublin and undertaken by unfamiliar examiners. Many students seemed to have thought that studying medicine in Cork was satisfactory but graduating there less so.

While information regarding the number of medical undergraduates in Cork at a given time is fairly easy to ascertain, it is (as outlined above) of limited value. Our knowledge of those who graduated is much more certain and also more relevant. Three students graduated in 1852, the first from QCC. Apart from 1854 when there seems to have been no medical graduates, Cork has produced doctors every year since. Numbers graduating have varied considerably: in the 1850s they were understandably small in the new college; by the end of the decade, they amounted to only thirty-one in all. There was a gradual increase during the 1860s, with more in the 1870s when an average of eighteen qualified per year.

In 1882, the Queen's University was dissolved and replaced by the Royal University of Ireland, which continued with three colleges. The reasons for the change were mainly political; one of the main objectives was to conciliate Catholics with whom the 'godless' Queen's University was never popular. It did not succeed in this to any extent but did confer its degrees on Queen's College students for the next twenty-eight years. For the first few years after its establishment, there was some optimism about its future and this was marked by a sudden increase in medical student numbers. This was, however, short-lived and was followed by a return to even fewer graduates than in the 1870s when it was realised that the final examination might be even more difficult for Cork students because of the increased dominance of Dublin examiners, which was deemed to militate against Cork candidates, and that the degree itself was no more attractive. Graduate numbers remained low for the rest of the century and indeed for the early 1900s as well. They increased only with the outbreak of World War I and a scarcity of doctors in Britain, with resultant employment opportunities there for new medical graduates from Cork and elsewhere.

When considering student and graduate numbers, two factors must be borne in mind. The first is that while numbers of both seem to us small, medical students were still the dominant group during the late 1800s in what was a small college. For example, in the 1899–1900 academic session, there were 135 medical students out of a total of 185, leading Murphy in his book on the college to comment that during this time the medical school, to a considerable extent, *was* the college.[2] A further point worth noting is that medical school numbers (and indeed all student numbers) at any one period of time depend on a variety of factors. These include the prevalent economic climate, the public's general perception of the value of a college or vocational education (which in Cork in the late nineteenth century does not appear to have been very high), the attitude of the people and of influential bodies (for example the Catholic Church) to a particular college, and, perhaps of greatest importance, the prospects (economic and social) which a particular career promises.

Gender

The Act of Parliament in 1879 by which the Royal University of Ireland was founded, opened the college's facilities to women and, in the 1885–86 session, the first women students were registered in the arts faculty. Medicine was not far behind and, in 1894, the first two women began their studies, both graduating in 1898. While Cork was not among the first medical schools to graduate women (Elisabeth Garret Anderson became a medical doctor at Apothecaries Hall in 1865), it did so sooner than either Trinity College Dublin or many British universities. The subject of women graduates in medicine in Cork is considered in some detail later, but it is worth noting that their admission to faculty caused surprisingly little difficulty. There were some reservations about their use of common dissecting room facilities and, in 1907, a new dissecting room for the exclusive use of women students was provided. They were few in number until the end of World War I and, in the early days, were largely non-Catholic. This would seem to have been because Catholic women were particularly pressured by Church authorities not to attend the college.[3]

Religion

Among the hopes of the founders of Queen's College was that it would cater equally for all religious beliefs. As Ireland was predominantly Roman Catholic, it was anticipated that a large majority of students would be of this religious persuasion. The opposition

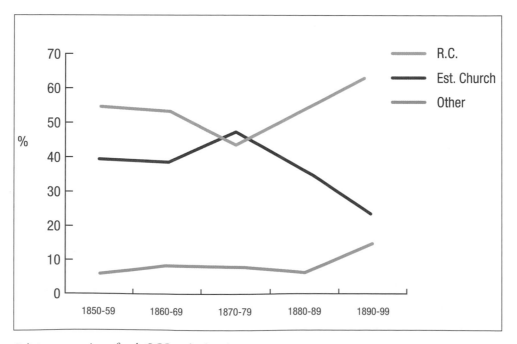

Religious persuasions of early QCC medical students

of the Catholic hierarchy to the college and their lack of participation in its governing structures threw this outcome into doubt. The Church's disapproval, however, never extended as far as absolute prohibition of attendance. In the event, Roman Catholics were in a small majority in the college in the nineteenth century, and this included medical students where they usually comprised about 54 per cent. In only one decade (1870–1879) were Catholics not in a majority. Of the non-Catholics, the Established Church accounted for 38 per cent of students while the rest were almost all Methodists, Presbyterians or Wesleyans. One Quaker, but no Jews, graduated in medicine in Cork during the nineteenth century.

While the proportion of Roman Catholics who graduated was much less than that of the total population, it was probably much closer to the proportion who were in a social and economic position to do so at the time. It would seem unlikely that the attitude of their hierarchy to the new college in Cork had a major influence on the decision of most Catholics about whether or not they would attend QCC. The lack of outright condemnation (such as declaring attendance a mortal sin or a cause for excommunication) combined with the absence of any real alternative for most to the Cork college, probably accounts for the fact that episcopal disapproval did not have a more decisive effect in an otherwise very compliant flock. That it did have some, however, is suggested by the fact that when the National University of Ireland (which was perceived to be more Catholic) was established in 1908, the student population became predominantly Catholic.

Birthplace and Social Background

Nearly all of the medical students and graduates of the nineteenth century were born in Ireland; only 3 per cent of the 679 graduates were born abroad. These were almost all the children of Irish servicemen posted abroad or of Irish emigrants. The Irish-born graduates fulfilled the aspirations of those who founded the college (they hoped that it would provide a third-level education for the people of Munster), in that 89 per cent of graduates were Munster-born. In fact, a majority (65 per cent) were from Cork city and county, with only a quarter from the rest of Munster. Interestingly, this preponderance of Munster, and more especially Cork-born students, has continued throughout the life of the college.

The social background of medical students and graduates is more difficult to ascertain with certainty but an educated guess can be arrived at with the use of a variety of sources. Certainly, they were not the children of the poor, none of whom were in a position to aspire to a third-level education. The majority were from the upper-middle classes, with a fair sprinkling of the sons of servicemen from the armed forces or otherwise. The children of the wealthy went to Oxford or Cambridge if they could, or otherwise to Trinity. Those who came to Cork were the sons of 'strong' farmers, owners of substantial shops or other businesses, professionals (such as doctors, lawyers and clergymen), together with the servicemen already mentioned. Then, as now, the children of doctors figured prominently among medical students at Queen's College Cork.

Society in the second half of nineteenth-century Ireland was relatively stable and it is fascinating to find successive generations from the same family graduating. Names such as Shinkwin, Pearson, Shipsey (from Cape Clear Island and Schull), McSwiney (Macroom) and Leader (North Cork) recur through the years, and it is of interest that members of these same families continue to practise medicine in Cork and elsewhere.

Destination and Career Choice

Throughout the nineteenth, and indeed for much of the twentieth, century, the numbers of Irish people graduating in medicine exceeded the perceived need for doctors in Ireland. From the founding of the school until the 1960s, a majority of Cork medical graduates found their permanent place of work abroad, and at no time was this more

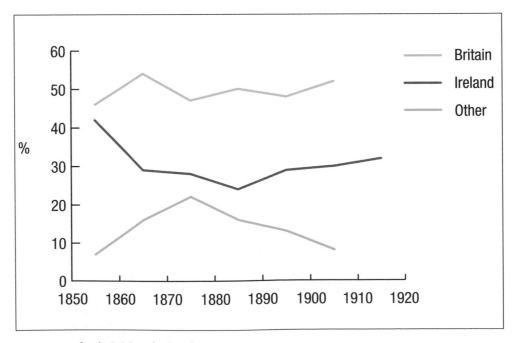

Destination of early QCC medical graduates

marked than in the college's first sixty years. Throughout this time, fewer than a third of those graduating settled in Ireland, more than half settled in Britain and a small but significant proportion elsewhere.

Of the graduates who settled in Ireland, the majority went in to general practice. The establishment of Dispensary Medical Officers by an Act of Parliament in 1851 created posts with a salary (albeit a small one), a pension, permanency and access to private practice. These proved a popular and much sought-after choice for Cork graduates who seemed to fill many of the vacancies in Munster, and an appreciable number in the rest of the country. A few held hospital medical officer posts in smaller centres and a few others became hospital consultants. In this regard, it has to be remembered that consultant posts were then very few in number compared to today, and those Cork graduates who attained them largely did so in their own city, where in time they filled the majority of such appointments. Similarly, when academic posts became vacant in Cork, local graduates were appointed most often. Consultant positions in Cork were not infrequently filled by the children of established medics in the city, a feature of Cork medicine which did not pass unnoticed by the general population in Cork or in medical circles elsewhere!

From 1850 to 1919, more than half of Cork medical graduates emigrated to and made their careers in Britain. While a majority served in the armed forces, a sizeable number worked in civilian practice. Most of these were in family medicine. At first, they worked almost exclusively in the London area but, from 1880 onwards, an increasing number settled elsewhere, usually in the larger cities and industrial areas. Less than two dozen worked in Wales and only two in Scotland. The dearth of Cork graduates north of the border can be explained in part by distance but probably much more by the fact that Scotland, like Ireland, traditionally produced more doctors than it could employ at home. Cork graduates in Britain who were not in the armed forces or general practice were few in number and worked in a variety of specialties, public health and psychiatry being the most common. There were clearly very few opportunities in hospital consultant posts.

The number and proportion of Cork medical graduates who enlisted in the British armed forces during the first half of the school's existence is remarkable. They exceeded those who stayed in Ireland. QCC together with Trinity College Dublin comprised two of the top five suppliers in the British Empire. While the Army Medical Service enrolled the largest number, the Royal Navy and, especially, the Indian Medical Service were also favoured. Protestant graduates were by no means the only ones to enlist; many recruits were the children of Catholic farmers, shopkeepers and professionals.

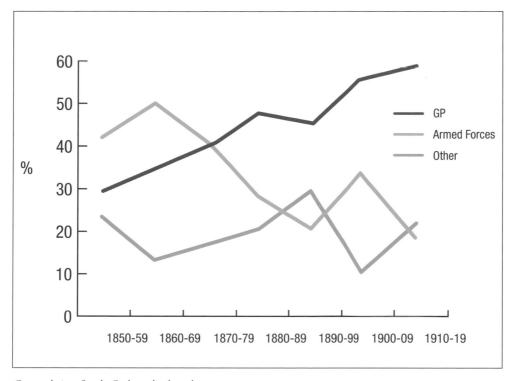

Career choice of early Cork medical graduates

Many attained high rank in their chosen service and some, after leaving the forces, stayed on in the country in which they served (be it India, China or South Africa), making valuable contributions both academically and administratively to those countries. The career of Robert Croly, who graduated in 1904 and joined the Indian army in which he served with distinction before going on to become Professor of Surgery in Madras, is such an instance.

The highest proportion of graduates joining the British armed forces was in QCC's first thirty years, when almost half of all medical graduates enlisted. From 1880 to 1919 some 25–30 per cent did so. The numbers of Cork graduates in the British armed forces during these years were such that they must have had a considerable impact, and the officers' quarters in Aldershot, Plymouth and Poonah probably resounded with Cork accents! Predictably, when Ireland gained independence in 1921, the numbers joining the British forces fell dramatically and did not recover.

Of the graduates who did not work in Ireland or Britain, the greatest number joined the Indian Medical Service which was a popular choice until the early years of the twentieth century. Those who chose otherwise were comparatively few in number (thirty-eight in all), but a very interesting group. Surprisingly perhaps, the USA was not the most popular location. South Africa and Australia were appreciably more favoured during the first seventy years of the college. Those who went to Australia (as well as the two brothers Whitton, who settled in New Zealand) often left home as surgeons on emigrant ships and decided to settle in the young colony. The emigrants to South Africa chose a wide variety of locations and specialties (surgeons, psychiatrists, general practitioners, mining medical officers), in their adopted country. While the USA did not become a popular destination until the 1950s, it was the choice of Michael Breen, one of the earliest graduates. He left Ireland in 1861, fought in the American Civil War and eventually became a family doctor in the USA.

Missionary work, particularly in Wesleyan mission hospitals, accounts for some of the more obscure postings. Other graduates went to unusual parts of the world because of family connections in those places. One of the most colourful overseas appointments at the time was that of Chief Sanitary Officer in Baghdad, which was held by Joseph McCraith towards the end of the nineteenth century. It can perhaps be partly explained by the fact that his family lived in Smyrna, even if both his surname and his given name, together with his Roman Catholic religion all suggest that his roots lay in Ireland rather than in that historic Turkish city.

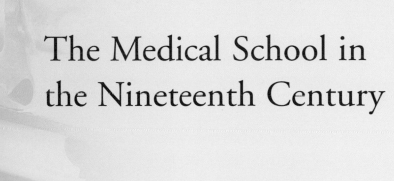

4

The Medical School in the Nineteenth Century

While the faculty members of the fledgling Cork medical school lacked the eminence of some of their better known Dublin counterparts (clinical, academic medicine in Dublin at this time had reached its apogee), they nevertheless included a number of men of medical substance and achievement. Denis Charles O'Connor, the first Professor of Medicine, had taught at one of the local medical schools before the college was established and was the first medical officer to the Cork Union Workhouse and later the Mercy Hospital. He graduated in Dublin but worked in Cork throughout a long career. (His thirty-nine years in the chair are the longest served by any Professor of Medicine.) He held many appointments, succeeded Bullen as dean, and was President of the British Medical Association when it met in Cork (see pp. 27–29). He died in office in 1888. His son (of the same name), who studied in Cork but interestingly did not graduate there, was his colleague as physician at the Mercy Hospital and also worked at the lying-in hospital, the lunatic asylum, as a dispensary doctor and as medical officer to the orphanage and to St Finbarr's Seminary.

The first Professor of Obstetrics and Gynaecology, Joshua Reuben Harvey, had a good obstetrical career but is perhaps better remembered for his presentation of a fine avian and mammalian collection to the college on his retirement. His successor, Henry Macnaughton-Jones, had a long, varied and interesting career. Its length is not surprising as he entered college at the age of fourteen (he was born in Cork in 1845, the year of the college's foundation), graduated when aged nineteen and quickly gained his surgical fellowship and postgraduate obstetrical qualifications by examination. He held appointments as demonstrator in anatomy, surgeon to the Cork Ophthalmic Hospital, physician to a Cork dispensary district and apothecary to the Cork Lunatic Asylum, all by the age of twenty-five. He founded the old Cork Eye, Ear and Throat Hospital when he was twenty-three and was co-founder of two further hospitals, the Cork Maternity Hospital and the Women and Children's (later Victoria) Hospital before he was thirty. He was also surgeon to the South Infirmary and physician to the Cork Fever Hospital by that time. As if these activities were not sufficient, he also founded the first branch of the British Medical Association in Ireland, was its secretary in Cork and it was he who suggested and organised the forty-seventh annual BMA meeting there.

He was appointed Professor of Midwifery in 1878 and his teaching efforts are described by one of his former students, Professor C. Y. Pearson, as 'indefatigable'.[1] Sadly, he held the post for only five years, apparently dissatisfied because he was not appointed Professor of Surgery (presumably in 1880 when Stephen O'Sullivan was appointed). He left Cork in 1883, still less than forty years old and moved to Harley Street in London where he practised with distinction; he died in 1918. He published widely and, while most of his published work was related to gynaecology, it also encompassed ENT, ophthalmology, anaesthesia and orthopaedic surgery. He was a member of a number of distinguished societies, and held high office in many.

Yet it is for none of these many activities that Macnaughton-Jones is best remembered in Cork, but rather as an author of verse and as a true and practical friend of his alma mater. He published collections of poems and popularised in verse (although he probably didn't himself compose) the college motto: 'Where Finbarr taught let Munster learn.' While the quality of his verse does not equal that of his gynaecological skills, his support for the Cork college was unrivalled. Instead of harbouring resentment when he left

Cork, he founded, and for many years chaired, the Old Corkonians graduates club in London, which interested itself in and gave much practical help to the college. It is also of interest that his son (of the same name) graduated at the Royal University of Ireland long after his father had left Cork, even though he studied at King's College and lived and practised in London. The life and work of the second Professor of Obstetrics and Gynaecology deserve wider acclaim than they have received to date.

Matters of concern to the medical faculty during its first half-century – apart from the great fire and its consequences – included buildings and accommodation for the school, but also the problems and fears posed when Queen's University was replaced by the Royal University in 1882. This was not a popular measure in Cork, particularly in the medical school where its powers to confer degrees on those who had matriculated at, but not necessarily attended, the college were deeply resented. Also, Cork students could be examined by a board of professors entirely external to their college but always containing at least one Dublin examiner. This they saw as unfair to them and favouring Dublin students. Finally, there was the real fear that the Cork medical school might be shut down (together with Galway which some deemed to be too small to be viable). This was much hoped for by some of the Dublin schools. All of these factors made QCC a rather unhappy and uncertain medical faculty for the last twenty years of the nineteenth century.

The BMA Meeting

A more joyful event was the holding of the forty-seventh annual meeting of the British Medical Association in Cork in August 1879. This was a big occasion for the small and still young school. It is well described by O'Rahilly (1949)[2] from whose account I have borrowed freely. It was the brainchild of Macnaughton-Jones who had recently been appointed a professor. He was highly regarded by the BMA whose Irish activities he pioneered, so when he invited them to Cork, they readily accepted. Although he was supported by appropriate executives and subcommittees, his tireless energy and boundless enthusiasm were major factors in the successful execution of what was for QCC, an enormous project.

Between 500 and 600 visitors came to Cork and it was said that London and Dublin were emptied of consultants. Other distinguished doctors came from more distant places such as Paris (including Professor Charcot), Berlin, Geneva, and even Chicago and New York. Town and gown fully supported the event and more than 2,000 guests attended the public opening reception, hosted in the college by the president, Dr W. K.

Sullivan. This seems to have been a splendid affair, held in fine weather with bands 'stationed at more than one point' and a well-spread buffet provided. Academic regalia was worn, carriages arrived at the new entrance on the Western Road, departing from the old one by the gaol. At the annual dinner of the BMA, which was held in the old Assembly Rooms on the South Mall, there were more than 300 guests, including the mayor, the college president and the High Sheriff of Cork. The college was lit electrically for the meeting, the first public installation of electric lighting in Cork. Virtually every musical, artistic, educational and scientific society in Cork made their contributions for the occasion.

The new president of the association was the Dean and Professor of Medicine, Dr Denis C. O'Connor. Papers presented and topics discussed have a very familiar ring to them as they included state medicine, medical education and the importance of psychological medicine.[3] A committee was even appointed to consider the desirability of adopting the metric system in Great Britain and Ireland. All lectures were in the Aula Maxima with numerous exhibitions in the Anatomical Room and the Pathological Museum. As the meeting was held in August, classes were not affected but students were allowed into the sectional meetings and the museums. Numerous excursions were arranged after the gathering to such predictable destinations as Blarney, the Blackwater Valley and Lismore Castle, Cork Harbour (by steamer and in yachts) as well as more long-distance trips to Glengarriff and Killarney.

The expenditure for the meeting was £1,500. It was said to have been 'one of the most successful meetings ever held by the British Medical Association'.

Towards the End of the Century

The last twenty years of the nineteenth century were rather uneventful ones for the medical faculty and somewhat depressing ones for the college as a whole. Then, as now, much of its success and progress was dependent on the president. In this regard, Queen's College Cork had rather mixed fortunes. Kane was succeeded by William Kirby Sullivan, a Corkman (the only one until the 1950s since when every president has come from the county), born in Dripsey, where his family owned a paper mill, and educated by the Christian Brothers in Cork. Like Kane, he was a chemist who distinguished himself in industrial chemistry and food production in Ireland. He was held in high regard in Dublin where the academic establishment was sorry to lose him to Cork. He worked hard during his seventeen years as president (1873–1890), in what were difficult times for the college. He had to contend with the difficulties which the establishment of the Royal University created, with inadequate funding, a continuing hostility to the college from Dublin and quite serious student misconduct. He oversaw the admission of the first women students (to whom he was sympathetic), was supportive of the medical school in its efforts to increase space and facilities (he was enthusiastic in advancing applied science in general), and overall was liked and esteemed by his staff and by the general public. He died in office in 1890 at the age of sixty-seven.

The next two presidents certainly did not enjoy the respect and popularity in which Sullivan was held. His immediate successor was James W. Slattery, a Tipperary man whose background was that of a 'spoilt priest' and classical scholar, even though he was an academic economist and a lawyer immediately before his appointment as president. This apparently broad background was evidently of little benefit as his six-year tenure was nothing short of catastrophic. His term was punctuated by frequent, prolonged absences, incompetence, very poor relationships with the staff, apparently chronic ill health and, to cap it all, bankruptcy. He was dismissed from his post by Queen Victoria in 1896 but because of severe illness did not leave the president's residence until his death in 1897, four months later. His tenure of office did no good whatever to an already depressed and insecure college with falling morale and student numbers.

The last thing that the college needed after Slattery's dismissal was another unsuccessful presidency but, unfortunately, this is what it got. Sir Rowland Blennerhasset was an establishment figure, born in Blennerville, County Kerry, to a Catholic gentry family. He was not the disaster that Slattery was but was undistinguished and non-productive. His reports about the college, which was probably at its lowest ebb at the time, were rosy and full of optimism. His aspirations and plans were almost grandiose, his achievements negligible. His absences from the college – often to mainland Europe and warmer climes – were multiple and prolonged. He finally resigned prematurely – although he was sixty-five – pleading that Cork's climate was unsuitable for his health. This had by now become a common plea from disgruntled and often unsuccessful presidents.

During these rather miserable and depressing times for the college, the medical school, while doing better than other faculties, also had its problems. Student numbers were low with few graduates. This was in the context of medical students making up about four-fifths of the total student numbers. During the years 1890–1905, the number of medical graduates per year averaged fewer than ten. This meant that more than half of the students who studied medicine in Cork at the time did not graduate at the Royal University of Ireland, disliking either its examinations, its degrees or both and preferring to gain their qualifications at one of the Royal Colleges, most often Dublin or Edinburgh.

Even with the small numbers, teaching, laboratory and demonstration accommodation was regarded as chronically inadequate. Even more important was the lack of chairs in physiology and pathology. It is strange then that despite these seemingly serious problems, opinions of the medical school seem to have been surprisingly positive. Blennerhasset, an incurable optimist with regard to the college, praised it highly. Visitors to the school were on the whole satisfied with what they found. Within Queen's College itself, there were few enough criticisms – although it should be remembered that the faculty was essential for the survival of the entire college, making up so many of its numbers, most of its prestige and a lot of the public's goodwill towards it. Whenever the closure of the college was seriously considered, the existence and perceived need for a medical faculty was one of the main arguments against such a measure. Furthermore, the products of the faculty, whether they graduated in Cork or elsewhere, appear to have been satisfactory. The majority worked either in family practice in Britain or in its armed forces (this was the time of the apogee of the British Empire), so that satisfactory service by graduates, whether in Britain, India or in some far-flung outpost, greatly helped the perceptions of those whose opinions of the school mattered most.

The general satisfaction with Cork medical graduates, wherever they worked, seems to have been well founded. Blennerhasset believed – apparently without any good evidence to support his views – that students from south Munster (whence most of the medicals came) were intellectually gifted, well above the average, but it is far more likely that they were good doctors because they had good teachers.

Successive professors of medicine at the end of the nineteenth and the beginning of the twentieth century were Edward Richard Townsend (1889–1897) and William Ashley Cummins (1897–1923). Both seem to have been superb clinicians and gifted teachers. Townsend died after only eight years in office but Cummins served for twenty-six years and was held in high esteem. He was a member of a Cork family, several generations of which practised and taught medicine in the city. One of his hospital appointments was that of physician to the Cork District Hospital (known as the Workhouse until 1898), and he did much of his clinical teaching there. He did a very valuable service to Cork academic medicine by securing recognition of the hospital for clinical teaching. He was apparently an outstanding bedside teacher as well as an astute clinician: a number of accounts exist of his remarkable abilities in both these regards.[4]

After the withdrawal from office of Bullen, the first professor, surgery settled into more peaceful times. Its fourth professor, Charles Yelverton Pearson, appointed at the turn of the century, had a distinguished and interesting career. He was a County Cork man, born in 1857 into a medical family, who graduated with distinction in Cork. Like many of the medical academics of the time, his path to the chair of surgery was a somewhat tortuous one, as he left the anatomy department to become Professor of Materia Medica and, later, lecturer in medical jurisprudence, holding at the same time surgical appointments at the North Infirmary, the Victoria Hospital, the Lying-In Hospital, and the Eye, Ear and Throat Hospital.

He attained considerable distinction from his involvement in a noted criminal trial of the time. This was known as the Dripsey murder case because it concerned the death of a Mrs Cross, wife of a retired army surgeon who lived in that area. Her death was not unexpected as she had been ill for some time but suspicions were aroused when her husband (who had been treating her himself and who, in her death certificate, had declared that she had died of typhoid fever), married their former governess, an attractive young woman who had recently left their employment, in London, ten days later. When he came back to Dripsey with his young bride, rumours spread and soon the police decided to exhume Mrs Cross' remains. Professor Pearson conducted the post-mortem examination and concluded that the deceased had died from arsenic poisoning. He based his opinion on, among other findings, a positive Marsh's test. This was probably the first occasion that the test had been used in such an important case and it brought both the test and Pearson considerable publicity. He was only thirty years old at this time and both his evidence and conduct at the trial received very favourable comment. Dr Cross was found guilty of murder and was hanged in Cork Gaol in January 1888.

Apart from all of this, Pearson was considered an outstanding surgeon and teacher. He was regarded as the link between pre-Listerian and the modern era of surgery in Cork. He was the author of a textbook (*Modern Surgical Technique,* 1906) and of many papers. He was Honorary Surgeon to the King in Ireland and lived to the age of ninety.

5

A New Century and a New President

While the new century at Queen's College opened with a certain air of despondency, the mood began to improve after the first few years. As so often happens, the reasons for this were multiple. The resignation of President Blennerhasset probably kindled some hopes of better things to come. More importantly, a number of commissions and other groups were active in trying to find a solution to the dissatisfaction with the existing university and college structures in Ireland. This was widely felt and of long standing. While much of it related to the disapproval of the now powerful Catholic Church with the existing arrangements, there was an overall feeling in the country that the university and college structures and administration could

Sir Bertram Alan Coghill Windle, President QCC/UCC, 1904–1919

and must be improved and the ongoing efforts to do so gave rise to new hopes. An improvement in the country's economy and a growing realisation of the benefits of third-level education also made the college perceive a more rosy future.

The appointment in 1904 of Sir Bertram Coghill Alan Windle as QCC's fifth president was undoubtedly the most important single factor in improving the image of the college. Windle was born in Mayfield in Staffordshire. His father was a Church of England vicar and his mother was the daughter of Admiral Coghill of Castletownshend in West Cork. He was educated at Repton, where he was said to have shown no industry, and at Trinity College Dublin, where he had a brilliant career. He graduated MB in 1891 with first place in his year and a gold medal and was awarded the MD two years later. He studied anatomy in Dublin for a short time, but soon moved to Birmingham where he was appointed pathologist to the General Hospital (where he is still remembered with respect) in 1882. He took the Chair of Anatomy at Queen's College Birmingham, in 1884.

This was an important time in the development of third-level education in Birmingham and Windle worked tirelessly in the development of the medical school. He played an important part in the establishment of the University of Birmingham where he was the first Dean of Medicine. He had no doubts about his role in all of this and Taylor quotes him as saying years later, 'Birmingham, I may say with all modesty, I made.'[1] While there, he built up a reputation as a superb anatomist, made many improvements in the teaching of anatomy, wrote a history of the medical school, completed his MD thesis (on the morbid anatomy of diabetes mellitus) and developed a deep interest in archaeology. He also converted to Roman Catholicism – having been born into the Church of England and become an agnostic early in his life – married Madoline Hudson with whom he had four children (two of whom died in infancy), and became deeply involved in social and charitable work as well as liberal politics. He was an examiner in anatomy in at least seven medical schools and was a member of the General Medical Council. He acquired a host of further degrees, including honorary doctorates of three universities, a Fellowship of the Royal Society and a knighthood. It was once said when he was being introduced that he had the first three letters of the alphabet before his surname and all the rest after it! He wrote extensively on anatomy, archaeology, religion and a variety of other subjects.

It was no wonder that the appointment of such an eminent and brilliant man as president of Queen's College Cork was acclaimed with enthusiasm in the struggling college. Perhaps, given the strong nationalist sentiments of the time, the welcome given by the student body was surprisingly warm. Three hundred of them – almost the entire student body – gathered in the quadrangle and marched to the railway station where they greeted Windle and his wife warmly and boisterously and followed them in procession back to the college where they received endless cheers, a welcoming address and bouquets from the women students (who were then very few in number).

Windle did not disappoint Cork's expectations and proved to be a great, if not the greatest, president. Without delay, he set about the task of changing and improving Cork from its position as little more than a not-very-successful technical school to that of an organised, well-run and thriving university college. Equally, he worked hard at ensuring that the college's relationships with the city and the community at large prospered. He achieved both of these aims in such a variety of ways that it is difficult to recount them with any brevity.

On the strictly medical scene, he organised separate chairs of anatomy and physiology, a long-awaited and much-needed improvement. As the Professor of Anatomy, John James Charles, was due to resign in 1907, Windle took the chair himself for two years and lectured four times a week – far more frequently than his full-time predecessor. He resigned the chair in order to establish and take the chair of archaeology for the next five years. Physiology was established in 1907 with D. T. Barry as the first professor. Windle initiated a professorship of pathology in 1910 and appointed the then lecturer, A. E. Moore to the post. He improved laboratory facilities in pathology and chemistry as well as library facilities for medicals.

Windle's contribution to the college in general was enormous. He cultivated relationships with students, in spite of having, it is said, a severe and distant manner, and greatly improved sports facilities, establishing the Mardyke Athletic Grounds. He had good relationships with staff, to whom he was very accessible. He promoted and took part in many social events with students, staff and the broader community outside college. He strove hard to foster and improve relationships between the college and Roman Catholic priests and bishops, succeeding in this to a degree, although never quite overcoming their aversion to women students. He fostered better administration, wrote admirable presidential reports and improved library facilities and services. Though he was constantly irritated by interference from and attempts at domination of the college and its affairs by various Dublin interests, he travelled to Dublin on average twice weekly in efforts to curb these.

Even with these staggeringly demanding activities, he succeeded in keeping up a flow of publications on a variety of subjects including anatomy, teratology, archaeology, religion and education. His publications in at least one year exceeded those of the rest of the staff combined. He also managed to maintain an active social life for himself and his wife: his first wife died towards the end of his time in Birmingham and he had married her cousin before he came to Cork. He took part in many other activities, particularly those associated with archaeology, which remained his abiding interest.

The University Question

While he was almost frenetically engaged in activities relating to the college, an even greater and more fundamental issue began to confront Windle's academic life. This concerned the entire question of university structures in the whole of Ireland which had become an increasing problem when the unsatisfactory nature of the Royal University of Ireland became evident. By the early years of the twentieth century, it was clear that Queen's College Belfast, was likely to secede and become an independent university. After much discussion (political and academic), the 1908 Irish Universities Act emerged. This proposed a separate Queen's University Belfast (which satisfied the northern unionists), and left Trinity College Dublin unchanged (which half-satisfied southern Protestants). It further proposed the establishment of a new National University of Ireland with constituent colleges in Dublin, Cork and Galway, which almost satisfied the Roman Catholic hierarchy even though they were slow to admit this.

Windle had, from the start, favoured a separate and independent University of Cork, hopefully almost free of what he saw as Dublin's interference and efforts at domination. While this had broad support in the college, and in Cork and, indeed, in Munster, it became part of a larger scenario which was to work to Windle's disadvantage and eventually to cause him to leave Cork. The advent of World War I started this process. Although Windle perceived himself as an Irish nationalist (and in many cultural matters he behaved as one), he was, in fact, English and pro-British. In Irish politics, he favoured John Redmond and was fully supportive of the British and their war efforts. Following the 1916 Easter Rising, there was a strong tide of Irish nationalism and some anti-British feeling in the college, and a fair measure of this was directed against Windle. In a complex (and perhaps not very rational) fashion, his campaign for an independent Cork university was seen by some as a pro-British stance and was therefore opposed quite vehemently. Alfred O'Rahilly, later to become president and a very powerful figure in UCC, led the opposition. He did so, it seems, partly for what he perceived as Irish nationalist reasons and partly because of considerable personal antipathy to Windle, whom he perceived as dictatorial. Predictably, O'Rahilly had the support of the NUI Senate which did not want the new university to fragment. There was a prolonged and often acrimonious struggle between the two factions between 1917–1919, and when a disillusioned and, by now, somewhat bitter Windle received an offer of a chair of philosophy in the University of Toronto in Canada (at the same time that he realised that his campaign for a separate university was lost), he quickly made up his mind to leave Cork and what he described as 'all its intrigues and worries'. He left for Canada in December 1919 with considerable feelings of bitterness, combined with regrets for what he perceived as his fifteen years of lamentable waste in Cork.

Windle continued to have a distinguished career in Canada, subsequently becoming Professor of Ethnology in Toronto. He died of bronchopneumonia at the age of seventy-one. Many regretted his leaving Cork but his departure in troubled times does not appear to have been regarded by a majority as the catastrophe it might once have seemed.

Bertram Windle was undoubtedly an outstanding president. His contribution to the medical school, while very significant, was of much less import than his overall impact on the college. At the time of his appointment, the outstanding medical dean and, more importantly, cultured and far-seeing polymath, found in Cork a medical school that needed some improvements and a college which required immediate and drastic reform and rejuvenation. Clearly, he got his priorities right. From Cork's point of view, he was, at the time of his appointment, the ideal man for the office of president. Sadly for him, he had ceased to be so at the time of his resignation, when his rather entrenched views and pro-British politics, together with the character and determination of his opponents, made his departure bitter but almost inevitable.

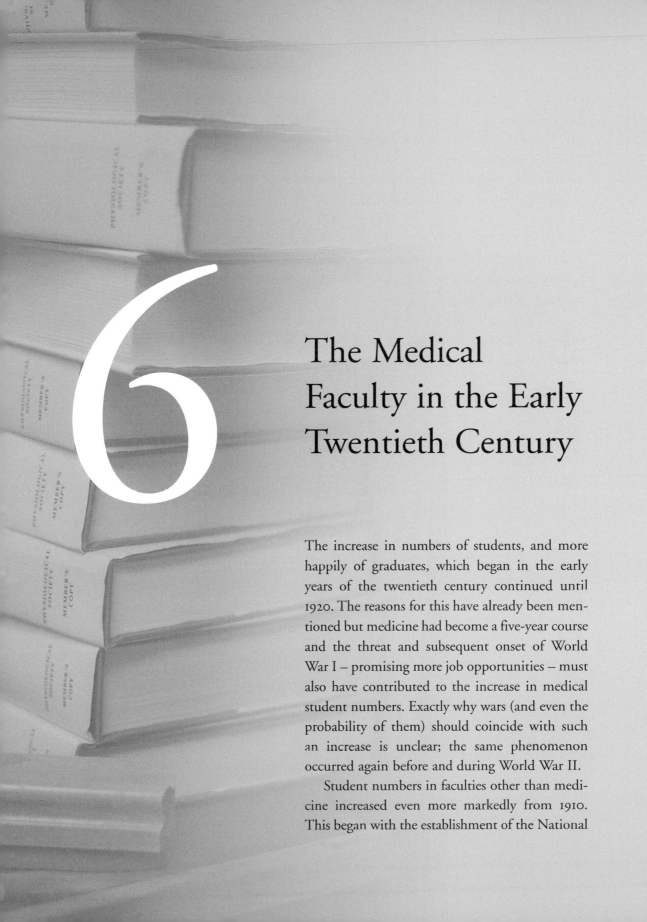

6

The Medical Faculty in the Early Twentieth Century

The increase in numbers of students, and more happily of graduates, which began in the early years of the twentieth century continued until 1920. The reasons for this have already been mentioned but medicine had become a five-year course and the threat and subsequent onset of World War I – promising more job opportunities – must also have contributed to the increase in medical student numbers. Exactly why wars (and even the probability of them) should coincide with such an increase is unclear; the same phenomenon occurred again before and during World War II.

Student numbers in faculties other than medicine increased even more markedly from 1910. This began with the establishment of the National

University of Ireland, when perhaps parents saw an end to the general disapproval which had been shown by Catholic Church authorities to the Queen's colleges strictly non-denominational approach to education. (The NUI was also non-denominational, in theory at least, but was clearly perceived by the Church as being less so.) The growth in numbers was greatest in the arts faculty and among women students, marking the beginning of the end of the numerical dominance of medical students in Cork. A further point worth noting is the quite marked disproportion between student and graduate numbers in medicine in any given year (for example, in 1916 there were about 300 medical students but only twenty-two graduates). At this time, the disparity was not due to students graduating elsewhere so there must have been very considerable wastage and also a sizeable number of 'chronic' students, for whom the medical faculty was famed right up to the 1950s.

During and immediately after the war years, an average of twenty-four students graduated in medicine each year. Interestingly, a smaller proportion of them joined the armed forces during this time than in pre-war years; the majority entered general practice in Britain where presumably there were many vacancies. About one-third of those graduating found work at home in Ireland.

Attitudes to Irish nationalism varied among both the students and staff of the medical faculty at this time. Windle and a number of other prominent members of staff (Professor D. T. Barry of physiology in particular), were enthusiastically pro-British during World War I, while, on the other hand, the 1916 Rising evoked strong nationalist sentiments among students. A few years later, many of the more actively nationalist students in the college were medicals and a number of stories of their exploits persist. These include the probably apocryphal one recounted by Murphy[1] of the anatomy student 'on the run' who, returning briefly to take his examination, was confronted at the practical with what he regarded as a difficult specimen. He placed his Wembley pistol on the table and quietly asked for 'an easier bone please, Sirs'.

It was a medical student, Flor O'Leary, who removed the Union Jack from the college tower during the post-1916 demonstrations and replaced it with the Tricolour. Sir Bertram Windle's departure in 1919 was certainly not marked by the show of emotion which greeted his arrival. It is probable, however, that a majority of students took little part in political activity at this time, or indeed subsequently.

Medicine in the Merriman Era 1920–1942

Immediately after Windle left Cork, the election of his successor took place, the first by the National University of Ireland, and completely new procedures were in place.

Election was by the senate of the university and three candidates who had been nominated by the governing body of UCC (having already been considered by the academic council of the college) were considered. Professor Patrick J. Merriman, the college registrar and its Professor of History was elected. He was a Dublin graduate and this was felt to give him a considerable advantage in the Dublin-dominated senate. His opponents were both from the Cork medical faculty as well as being Cork graduates. Professor David Barry (physiology) and Professor P. T. O'Sullivan (medical jurisprudence and later medicine) were felt to have little support outside of Cork and, in any case, Barry was unrepentantly pro-British and anti-Sinn Féin. The election reflected the geographic and academic/political overtones of the time, and was to prove an accurate predictor of what was going to characterise many future NUI senate elections for academic posts at UCC.

Merriman was not a dominant figure; his long tenure in office was characterised by much inaction and, after Windle's eventful presidency, was somewhat anticlimactic. In the medical faculty also, the 1920s and 1930s were rather uneventful times. Student and graduate numbers dropped sharply in the 1920s from the comparatively high numbers which characterised the war and immediate post-war years. Entry to the British armed forces fell dramatically and the majority of graduates went into general practice in Britain with less than a third finding work in Ireland, mostly as dispensary medical officers. Fewer than 7 per cent of graduates went elsewhere, mostly to colonial medical services, a few to mission work and the rest to a variety of unusual careers, such as prison medical officers, railway and mining doctors, hospital medical officers, and psychiatrists, in strange and unexpected places. The small but, by now, steady number of female medical graduates not infrequently became public health officers, hospital medical officers or family doctors in Britain. In the 1920s, only 10 per cent of Cork graduates became consultants, most often in their native cities or towns; by the 1930s this had increased to 18 per cent and subsequent to this there was a further increase to between one-quarter and one-third of those graduating.

Significant academic staff changes took place in the medical faculty during the 1920s in that all three major clinical chairs changed hands. The highly respected Ashley Cummins, Professor of Medicine, died in office in 1923, and his equally regarded surgical colleague Charles Yelverton Pearson retired in 1927, happily living for a further twenty years. The long-serving (forty-two years) Professor of Obstetrics and Gynaecology, Henry Corby, left office in 1925; he was a native of Cashel who had been High Sheriff for Cork in 1904 and had been expected by many to become president when Windle was appointed. All three belonged to the old Cork medical establishment while their

J. J. Kearney, Professor of Obstetrics and Gynaecology, 1926–1948

successors represented in many ways the face of the new Irish state. The new appointees were all Cork graduates, all Roman Catholics and all held positions in the Bon Secours and Mercy hospitals (and mostly, in many others as well!), where much private practice was carried out. The new Professor of Medicine, P. T. O'Sullivan, was a native of Cork city. He was a very busy practitioner and an excellent didactic lecturer, but held the chair for less than ten years, dying in office in 1932. John Dundon had a brilliant undergraduate career, taught chiefly at the North Infirmary and was Professor of Surgery for thirteen years until 1941.

Of the three, by far the most interesting was J. J. Kearney who became Professor of Obstetrics and Gynaecology in 1926. He was a native of West Cork, from a farming background and was a man of quite extraordinary versatility and industry. After an outstanding undergraduate career, he gained an MD with Gold Medal and a Diploma in Public Health with first-class honours, both by examination in the same year. He followed this with an Edinburgh Fellowship in surgery and took postgraduate courses in tuberculosis in Dublin and in pathology in London, where he was a clinical assistant in obstetrics and gynaecology in two hospitals. For a brief period, he was a family doctor in Rosscarbery, West Cork, but soon moved to hospital practice in Cork. There, he was surgeon/gynaecologist to three general hospitals (South Infirmary, Mercy and Bon Secours), professor/obstetrician to the Erinville Maternity Hospital and physician to St Patrick's Hospital, as well as an advisor in assurance. He had great manual dexterity in spite of losing a finger in a farming accident in his youth; it was said that his hands had been blessed by the Pope! His range of surgical and obstetrical skills seemed limitless and he combined surgery, gynaecology, obstetrics, ENT surgery and general practice without seeming effort and with much success. He had an easy and affable manner, great kindness and a reputedly prodigious memory for patients, with whom he was hugely popular. His enormous workload left him little enough time for his teaching activities and none for research but he was well liked by students to whom he was kind and courteous. He retired from the chair of obstetrics and gynaecology in 1948. Three of his sons became consultants in Cork; one of them, William, succeeded him as professor. The family continues to thrive medically in Cork and elsewhere. He was a medical phenomenon, whom it will never be possible to replicate and he will remain a legend in Cork medicine.

In anatomy, during his brief tenure as professor, Windle appointed his demonstrator, Dr Denis Patrick Fitzgerald, lecturer and then resigned the chair in his favour two years later. Professor Fitzgerald, known to all as 'Dinny Pa' spent nearly all his working life in the Department of Anatomy, resigning in 1942 after thirty-three years in the chair.

His writings were quite extensive, some in anatomy and quite a number on the history of old Cork and of the medical school.

The so-called 'minor' clinical subjects, ophthalmology and otology, psychiatry, medical jurisprudence, hygiene, materia medica, and therapeutics, tended to be largely one-man departments and very part-time at that. The first Professor of Ophthalmology and Otology was Arthur W. Sandford. He was appointed in 1910, having been lecturer for twenty years before this, and held the chair until his resignation in 1926. He organised the building of the old Eye, Ear and Throat Hospital, was highly regarded in his specialty in Britain and married the author, Lady Mary Carbery, who wrote affectionately of him. He is said to have worn a different suit every day! He was succeeded by Vernon O'Hea-Cussen who headed the department, again first as lecturer and later as professor, for many years. Psychiatry was taught by a lecturer who was, almost of necessity, the Resident Medical Superintendent of the Cork Mental Hospital, while the teaching of hygiene was similarly almost always entrusted to the city's Chief Medical Officer of Health.

Both medical jurisprudence, and materia medica and therapeutics were, for the last quarter of the nineteenth century and for much of the first half of the twentieth, taught by clinicians who often subsequently became professors of medicine or surgery. Two professors of medicine (P. T. O'Sullivan and James M. O'Donovan) and one of surgery (C. Y. Pearson), had been professors or lecturers in jurisprudence before moving on, while two professors of surgery (Pearson and Dundon) had previously been professors of materia medica.

In all of the above clinical departments, the professors held consultant appointments in a number of hospitals and almost invariably had busy private practices as well (J. J. Kearney, for instance had a very large private obstetrical practice which he carried out assiduously as he did his many other clinical duties). Time for academic duties was of necessity limited and these consisted solely of lecturing and bedside teaching. There was no clinical or other research and little if any career guidance. Bedside teaching was, in fact, mostly carried out by clinical teachers – hospital consultants who did not have academic appointments and who were recompensed after a fashion by clinical fees paid by students to the individual hospitals. Fortunately, many of them were splendid teachers, very conscious of the strictures imposed by the Hippocratic Oath with regard to teaching. Their monetary rewards were pitifully small and indeed the salaries paid to clinical professors and lecturers were by modern standards also derisory. It is probable that these academic posts were sought after so avidly chiefly because of the status and distinction they conferred. Pre-clinical academic posts were full-time ones and only moderately recompensed. In these departments, some efforts at research were made but an almost total lack of research funding made these attempts difficult and unsatisfactory.

In retrospect, one wonders how a medical school like Cork could have been deemed satisfactory in such circumstances and concludes that it may well have been because matters were not all that better in larger and better known schools.

The Students

College life for undergraduate medical students – there were no postgraduates – in the later 1920s and early 1930s cannot have been exciting. Numbers were small and very few women graduated. In the other faculties, the decline in numbers was less and of shorter duration. By the mid-1930s medical student numbers again increased, not due to any improvement in the Irish economic situation (which remained depressed), but because of more job opportunities in Britain. Women students and graduates again increased in number and comprised about a quarter of the total.

During this time, two unrelated, non-academic phenomena played important positive roles in making undergraduate life more tolerable for medicals. The first of these was rugby football, the other was the College Rag.

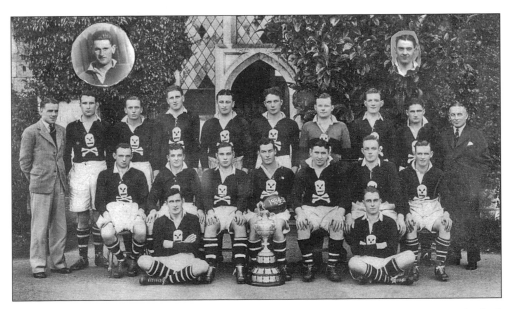

UCC, Munster Senior Rugby Cup Winners, 1934–35. Medical students are in the majority and include: (back row) fifth from left, Jack Russell, fourth from right, William Kearney (later obstetrics) and, seated W. M. O'Sullivan (Killarney), team captain

Rugby in Ireland in the 1920s and 1930s was a decidedly minority sport, yet in UCC it was popular and fashionable and had been so for many years. This was largely because many of the students came from upper-middle-class schools where rugby was played, but the game was also favoured by many of those in authority in college. Windle, for instance, was an enthusiastic rugby supporter. Even in the early years of the state when nationalism was a powerful force, Gaelic games did not attract great support, especially in the medical faculty (even if Professor George Sigerson was a Cork medical graduate). The GAA was much more closely associated with the new faculty of dairy science which was established in 1926 and whose students had a largely farming background, while a majority of any UCC rugby team's members were medical students. When the comparatively small numbers of available talent is considered, the success of college rugby teams and of their individual members is remarkable. For a time in the 1930s, the college had three internationals on their senior team, and names like Jack Russell and Charlie Teehan, then both medical students, are still spoken of with reverence. Membership of the senior rugby team conferred a respect and popularity which greatly exceeded that accorded to any academic distinction.

The annual College Rag was another important social outlet for a student body whose spare-time activities were, for a variety of reasons, much more restricted than those of their counterparts today. Held in late spring before the pressure of summer examinations became too urgent, the Rag was the greatest non-academic event of the year. Its stated objective was to raise money for charity (which it did effectively), but more importantly for students it provided a legal (mostly) means of expressing inventiveness, ingenuity and high spirits. Students (all male as the females did not participate directly but provided a valuable back-up role) gathered in the quadrangle, bedecked in a wide and colourful variety of costumes and devices depicting current national and international social, political and otherwise newsworthy events and situations. Certain female film stars of the time, including Mae West, were popular models to depict, while local and national politicians and other celebrities of the time were frequently the butt of clever and often cynical mimicry. When it had been inspected by amused and admiring staff members and female students, the colourful if rather heterogeneous spectacle went in procession to the city centre where the participants dispersed and spent the rest of the day in a wide variety of extroverted, often wild but almost invariably good-humoured activities. Though collecting for charity at the same time, their somewhat manic behaviour was often helped by alcoholic stimulants. Medical students, particularly the older and more experienced ones (and there were in those days a fair sprinkling of these) tended to be prominent and particularly inventive in Rag-day activities. Informal 'doctorates'

Top: College Rag participants being inspected by President P. J. Merriman in the late 1930s. Bottom: College Rag participants, Grand Parade, Cork c.1940

were sometimes conferred on well-known local eccentrics in elaborate ceremonies in St Patrick's Street and, with the advent of World War II, the hastily constructed air-raid shelters in the city centre provided ideal platforms from which to flaunt some of the more daring impersonations.

The citizens of Cork were mostly tolerant, mildly amused and financially supportive of the Rag. The 1943 event, however, seems to have gone beyond accepted levels of tolerance and decorum with the Society of St Vincent de Paul declaring that it would not in future accept badly needed funds gleaned from Rag activities. The new president, Alfred O'Rahilly, regarded by many as somewhat austere and intolerant anyway, promptly banned future Rags, much to the regret of most students and so ended, in its original form, an annual event which was regarded by many as an intrinsic and enriching part of college life.

7

Medicine in the Mid-Twentieth Century

World War II dominated much of the 1940s in the medical faculty. Student and graduate numbers had already begun to rise sharply from the mid-1930s and the 1940s saw about 600 medicals graduate from Cork. This was the largest number in any decade from the foundation of the college until the 1970s. With overall student numbers also increasing, there were 1,100 students attending UCC in the mid-1940s. Females now comprised a quarter of the medical graduates. The pre-medical year had been introduced in the late 1930s so that medicine had become a six-year course of studies. For the first half of the 1940s, more than half of those graduating went to Britain where, because of the war, jobs were plentiful. From 1945 however, fewer than 40 per cent did so and the tendency to migrate elsewhere – chiefly to the USA – began. Similarly, less than 40 per cent of Cork graduates at this time remained in or returned to Ireland. Just over half became family doctors and a quarter consultants. Life for medical students was not easy. Money was in short supply, rationing limited many activities, summer work (never a big factor in student life up to then anyway) was unobtainable except in the turf bogs and a more austere and rigid atmosphere began to permeate extra curricular activities in college.

This latter feature of college life was, in part at least, due to the accession to the presidency in 1943 of Professor Alfred O'Rahilly. A Kerryman by birth, O'Rahilly was a Jesuit student at the beginning of his adult life and a Holy Ghost priest at the end of it. He was appointed Professor of Mathematical Physics in 1917 and succeeded Merriman as registrar in 1919. He was one of the main anti-Windle agitators before the latter's departure from Cork and did not have the best of relationships with Merriman either, complaining about the length of his presidency and his relative inactivity in the post. O'Rahilly could certainly not be accused of inactivity as he was a man of extraordinary energy who sought to, and succeeded, involve himself in almost every aspect of college life. This, he dominated for all of the 1940s and much of the 1950s and left a long shadow. He was a brilliant polymath, writing and speaking authoritatively on a wide variety of subjects, religious, moral, philosophical, political and scientific. He was austere in his attitude to college life and a guardian of morals to an unrealistic and almost ludicrous degree. (Tales of his pinching ladies' legs in one of his many per-ambulations around the quadrangle, to find out if they were wearing stockings persist, even if it is difficult to confirm them.) One of his many dicta regarding student behaviour was that it was a breach of discipline for them to frequent public houses and places of low repute, a rule which was never enforceable or enforced. Furthermore, women students were forbidden to smoke in the college grounds and were told that they must not lie on the grass.

His contributions to UCC were, however, multiple, important and lasting. He founded the Department of Electrical Engineering, greatly improved the student restaurant, health and library facilities, acquired the neighbouring gaol for the college and established the adult education system. In many other ways, he altered the perception of the college in the eyes of the state, the Church and the general public. He wielded huge influence both within the college and outside it and his deep religious convictions and conservative views permeated all levels in an already conservative institution.

O'Rahilly seems to have made few changes nor indeed taken great interest in academic medical matters, notwithstanding the fact that medical students still comprised over one third of the college total. He did, however, interest himself greatly in the disputes of the late 1940s and early 1950s concerning the role of the state in medicine and particularly in what he saw as its attempts to interfere in medical education.[1] His stances on both issues were totally predictable. When it was perceived in the early 1950s that the medical school's very existence was threatened (see below), he took what he considered to be practical, energetic and important measures to counter this but, in fact, little of practical importance was achieved by college with regard to this threat during his presidency which ended with his retirement in 1954.

Some Notable Professors

Two important and interesting appointments to the medical faculty were made in the early 1940s. John Dundon was replaced as Professor of Surgery by Patrick Kiely in 1941 and in the following year Michael A. MacConaill succeeded Denis P. Fitzgerald in anatomy.

Professor Kiely, or 'P. Kay' as he was widely known (a title which he invented himself as a golfing identity) came from a West Waterford farming family, graduated in 1920 and took an active part both in the War of Independence and the subsequent Civil War. In spite of these extracurricular activities, he had a distinguished undergraduate career and after graduation, quickly gained the MD and MCh degrees, followed by a London FRCS. He was an intrepid surgeon whose training was almost entirely local, in the anatomy department and in the South Infirmary, where he was a house physician and radiologist. He had a phenomenal memory and his teaching, both bedside and didactic, was distinctive and much liked. His Waterford accent, endless lists of clinical facts and many anecdotes, were much mimicked. He was quick-tempered as a surgeon but regained his composure equally rapidly. He drove himself hard; as well as a busy surgical life, he played a good game of golf, gambled courageously and was

Patrick Kiely, Professor of Surgery 1941–1967

an enthusiastic and often successful racehorse owner. He was very popular with students, patients and colleagues and was generous to a fault. He took a full part in college administration, spending many years as college governor, NUI senator and later as faculty dean. In spite of a life seemingly full of hard work and stress, he lived to over one hundred years and walked and played golf to a great age.

Michael Aloysius MacConaill who held the chair of anatomy from 1942 until 1973, was an equally idiosyncratic but very different character to 'P. Kay'. A northern nationalist, a Queen's graduate and an anatomist of repute, he was one of the medical faculty's few polymaths. Eloquent in a number of languages, he had a lively interest in a wide variety of subjects as well as anatomy, including philosophy, archaeology and history. He had also a passionate pride in his membership and involvement in the national defence forces. He was an irrepressible speaker on a wide variety of subjects at multiple college and other meetings, and seemed to take in his stride the many changes which occurred in the medical faculty during his long membership of it.

M. A. MacConaill, Professor of Anatomy, 1942–1973

Less colourful but certainly no less important in academic medical affairs during the 1940s and 1950s were the O'Donovan brothers, William J. and James M. The former, popularly known as Billy, was the elder of the two even though he graduated later, as he was in the civil service for some years before studying medicine. He was appointed Professor of Pathology in 1941 and Dean of Medicine in the same year. He held the deanship for sixteen years, including the troubled 1950s when it cannot have been an easy task, particularly as he was, at the same time, professor of an understaffed department and consultant pathologist to the South Charitable Infirmary.

W. J. O'Donovan, Professor of Pathology, 1941–1965, Dean of Medicine, 1941–1957

James Michael O'Donovan became Professor of Medicine in 1932. He was a fine clinician and a clear and precise clinical teacher and lecturer. He was held in considerable awe by his students and was greatly feared as an examiner. His main appointment was as physician to the North Charitable Infirmary but he also had a considerable private practice in other hospitals. While held in great respect because of his clinical and teaching skills, he had a rather autocratic manner and was somewhat naive and intolerant as a medical politician. These latter attributes led him into considerable difficulties in the 1950s. He was, nevertheless, a very important figure in Cork medicine for nearly three decades.

An Unsatisfactory Situation

In spite of these talented senior teachers, in the 1940s the Cork medical school was neither successful nor distinguished. Although student numbers increased with the war, the faculty did not modernise as many others did at the war's end. Even though the pre-clinical departments were understaffed, they functioned reasonably well and most of the defects lay in the clinical areas. There, all the weaknesses of the 1930s persisted, with minimal academic staffing by very part-time appointees whose main involvement was elsewhere in non-teaching activities, particularly private practice. This meant that little other than basic teaching and lecturing was carried out. Again, bedside teaching was adequate due in considerable part to the largely selfless efforts of the clinical teachers. Clinical academic departments did not exist and there was no clinical research. Furthermore, there was no effective career guidance and no postgraduate academic activity. Apart from the visits of external examiners (who generally found the performance of students in the final examinations satisfactory), there were few contacts with medical schools outside of Ireland and clinical lectures from visiting speakers were few or non-existent.

This state of affairs continued through the late 1940s and early 1950s. While it might have been tolerated in the 1930s and earlier, when perhaps things were not very different elsewhere, by 1950 things had to alter. After World War II, major changes were taking place in clinical medical education, particularly in Britain and in the USA. In the former, where many Cork graduates hoped to find work, the National Health Service had been established in 1948 and, at the same time, there was a growing emphasis on full-time clinical teaching. With the war over, the number of native young doctors available for civilian work increased markedly with resultant fewer opportunities for Irish graduates. In the USA, which was becoming an increasingly popular destination for newly qualified UCC doctors, there was a growing emphasis on the importance of laboratory and radiological facilities in undergraduate medical education. This too was worrying for Cork where neither specialty was well developed. The virtual absence of specialisation in such subjects as paediatrics, cardiology and the neurosciences posed further problems: in Cork most 'specialists' at this time were also general practitioners. While some of these inadequacies were adverted to occasionally (as in Professor J. M. O'Donovan's conferring speech of 1952),[2] they did not seem to cause widespread anxiety and little enough was done about them.

Two Revealing Visitations

The reports from two visitations in the mid-1950s fully exposed the faults and limitations of medical teaching in Cork at that time. A scathing report followed a visit from the American Medical Association in 1953,[3] when aspersions were cast particularly on the standards and teaching in the Cork medical faculty. Many faults were found and laboratory and radiology teaching services were said to be grossly inadequate. A report in 1954[4] following a visitation from the British-based General Medical Council was, in its way, even more critical, particularly of the state of clinical teaching. The two visitors had been external examiners in Cork and expressed surprise 'that the students do so well when clinical instruction is in a state which we can only describe as chaotic'.

The latter visitation was not helped by the inability of the most senior professor, James M. O'Donovan (medicine), to accompany the visitors because he had resigned from the staff of the North Infirmary in protest of the fact that he had 'no clinical charge of teaching beds'. He also resigned from the chair of medicine on account of 'the backward state of clinical teaching in Cork and the entire absence of interest not to speak of control, exercised by the College'.[5] The North Infirmary accepted his resignation but UCC persuaded him to retain the chair.

A further embarrassment for the college were the twin findings by the visitors that St Finbarr's Hospital, where much of the clinical teaching was by then carried out, was not a recognised teaching hospital and had no faculty representation, while at the Mercy Hospital, where two physicians and four surgeons were recognised as clinical teachers 'no teaching whatever took place'. (This was not entirely correct as female students carried out residencies in the hospital during the period 1930–1960). The anomaly of St Finbarr's lack of recognition was soon solved by the creation of an amendment to the 1953 Health Act, but the situation at the Mercy took much longer to correct. Also, in response to the visitors' criticisms, statutory lectureships were created in pharmacology at the college and in the clinical subjects at the teaching hospitals, in the hope of better integrating the latter into the academic scene. Nevertheless, the outlook for the medical school was at best uncertain and this was confirmed by gloomy utterances by both the retiring president, O'Rahilly in 1954,[6] and his successor, H. St J. Atkins in 1955.[7] Many states in the USA did not recognise Cork medical qualifications; happily Massachusetts was a notable exception and attracted a number of Cork graduates. In Britain, worthwhile junior posts became more difficult to obtain and the Cork medical school was taken less than seriously by some, as instanced by Richard Gordon in his book *Doctor at Large*[8] 'medical degrees are readily obtainable at the college of apothecaries in Cork'.

Students and Graduates

Students of the 1940s differed little from those of the previous twenty years except that they were more numerous. Both student numbers and their origins changed in the 1950s. By the middle of that decade, Irish-born medical students declined in number. How much of this was due to the economic depression of the time, to diminished employment prospects both at home and abroad or to the altered perception of the school in the public view is difficult to evaluate, and it may well have been due to a combination of all three factors. To some degree, the fall in the number of Irish-born students was compensated for by the arrival of students from other countries; a majority came from the

USA but a number came from a variety of other origins, including the African continent, the Caribbean islands and Poland. In spite of these additions, overall numbers fell and reached their nadir in the early 1960s.

The destination of graduates also changed. From the opening of the school, graduates largely spent their careers in Britain but, in the 1950s, increasing numbers went elsewhere, chiefly to the USA but also to Canada and Australia. This was in small part due to the increased number of foreign-born students but much more because Britain in the 1950s was economically stressed and, at the same time, amply provided for by its own young medical graduates, while the New World was booming and offered many opportunities to Irish doctors.

In Britain, most Irish immigrant doctors went into general practice, but this was not the case in the newer countries. In these, the demand for consultants was greater and specialist training was much less rigid. As a result, in the late 1950s and early 1960s, a greater proportion of Cork graduates became specialists rather than general practitioners. In those years, however, it must be remembered that graduate numbers were small and economic and social circumstances somewhat unusual. By the middle of the 1960s, family medicine had again become the most popular choice.

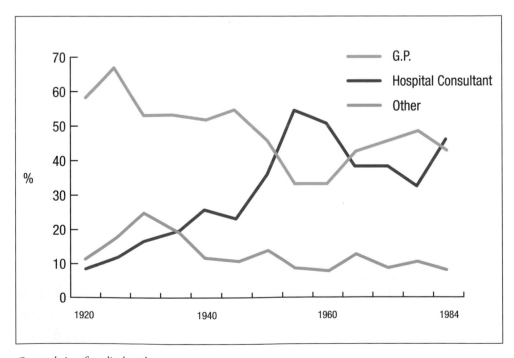

Career choice of medical graduates, 1921–1984

8

Major Events in the Early 1960s

A Full-Time Clinical Chair

Professor James M. O'Donovan resigned the chair of medicine in 1958 at the age of sixty-five. His later years in the post had been eventful and troubled and, following his departure, there was much discussion about the future of the professorship. Dr Andrew J. Whelton, his consultant colleague and lecturer at St Finbarr's Hospital, became acting professor and it was eventually decided that the chair would become a full-time one. This meant that the appointee would have beds in one hospital only, would be jointly appointed, employed and recompensed by the hospital authority and UCC, and would be precluded from engaging in private practice. These conditions meant realistically that the clinical section of the post would be in St Finbarr's Hospital and that the clinical employer would be the local health authority, as neither of the infirmaries would have had the requisite number of beds nor the facilities to accommodate such a department.

The concept of a full-time clinical chair, while by then the norm in Britain, was a new one in the Republic and by no means universally approved of. It was viewed with some suspicion by the local voluntary hospitals as a further step in the erosion of their already waning influence. At St Finbarr's Hospital, where the existing clinical consultants were all part-timers with multiple hospital appointments and private practices, the proposed addition of a completely new type of clinical colleague naturally caused much pause for thought, while, in the same hospital, it was predictably greeted with enthusiasm by the small number of recently appointed, full-time staff (laboratory and radiology consultants). At national level, the Irish Medical Association had many misgivings about the post, viewing it with some hostility as they saw it as further government involvement in and control of consultant posts. They were also suspicious of consultant posts without private practice; and, at that particular time, they were at odds with the Department of Health about the latter's handling of a consultant post elsewhere.

In the medical faculty, the pre-clinical members approved of the concept while among the clinicians attitudes were mixed and reflected to some degree the views of individual teaching hospitals. Faculty as a whole supported it, however, as indeed did the academic council and governing body. At executive level, both the UCC president, Harry (Henry St J.) Atkins, and the health authority CEO, Walter McEvilly, were enthusiastic proponents.

By mid-1960, the joint post was finally agreed and advertised. After a very cumbersome appointment process (involving an interview, followed by consideration and approval of the results by the Minister for Health, all electing bodies of UCC and the Senate of the National University of Ireland), the successful candidate, Denis O'Sullivan (the author) was appointed in July 1961 and took up duty in August.

In spite of the years of consideration of the post, virtually no support for the new appointee had been arranged and, on arrival, I found myself without an office or a secretary but entrusted with the care of seventy-six acute in-patients (all females as there was no provision for male beds). There were, as well, normal out-patient duties and I was helped only by a registrar and housemen. At academic level, there were three very part-time lecturers (the senior physicians at the teaching hospitals) and no other support or assistance.

The almost total absence of even rudimentary necessities for a new department at first sight seemed like culpable neglect; in fact it soon became apparent that much of it was due to the almost total lack of knowledge of the requirements of a modern department of medicine, combined with negligible financial provision by both the university and the health authority for anything beyond the professor's actual salary. While the responses to repeated requests, and indeed pleading, for the provision of the most fundamental facilities were painfully slow and inadequate, the ability to carry on at all was made possible by co-operative administrators together with friendly and sympathetic medical colleagues and superb nursing staff.

A Further Visitation and a New Hospital

While the process of appointing a Professor of Medicine was at last reaching a conclusion, a further visitation of the medical schools of the Republic by GMC visitors took place in June 1961. This was a sequel to the adverse findings of the 1954 visitors and, while it was appreciably more encouraging,[1] it still had much to criticise in the Cork faculty and many recommendations to make.

The visitors found the division of students in equal numbers between each of the two small voluntary hospitals and the much larger St Finbarr's Hospital incomprehensible. The departments of pathology and paediatrics came in for harsh criticism, the visitors insisting in their recommendations that each should be based on the clinical facilities at St Finbarr's and headed by full-time professors with headquarters at this hospital. Throughout the report, they stressed the need for modern clinical and laboratory facilities in a large, new teaching hospital, jointly planned and administered by closely co-operating university and health authorities. While it found that the clinical material at St Finbarr's was satisfactory, it reiterated throughout the report that the aged hospital 'retains the essential structure of a large workhouse infirmary of the last century'.

On a more positive note, the visitors acknowledged that many efforts had been made to implement the recommendations of their 1954 predecessors. Importantly for Cork, they condemned out of hand proposals being considered at the time by the Commission on Higher Education that medical education should be centralised in one or other of the colleges of the National University of Ireland, possibly leading to the cessation of the Cork medical school. They stressed how important the continuation and expansion of the school was to the community of nearly 1 million people in Munster. They recommended 'as strongly as we can that the University College of Cork should make urgent recommendations to the Minister of Health concerning the need for a new Regional Teaching Hospital of 600 or more beds to replace outdated accommodation at St Finbarr's Hospital'.

St Finbarr's Hospital in the 1960s

The idea of a new general hospital in Cork was far from new. As long ago as 1936, the then Department of Local Government and Public Health recommended that a new central hospital be built under the control of the South Cork Board of Public Assistance, a precursor of the Health Authority. There were to be no fewer than 300 beds as well as an extern department, and the hospital was to be so designed as to permit easy extension (to 600 beds). A site at Wilton was acquired in 1938 and the initial all-in cost was estimated at £200,000. By 1939, this had risen to £473,540 which the board considered exorbitant. Interminable wrangling about the cost and other details went on and no further progress was made until 1948 when Dr Noël Browne became Minister for Health. He proposed that a 400-bed hospital be built and planning was resumed. A change of government and rising costs resulted in a series of deferrals and, by 1957, the prospects for a 500-bed hospital together with a dental school looked grim, even though extensive planning for both had taken place. To quote the Cork *Evening Echo* 'the dream was ended, the prospect was abandoned'.[2]

By 1961, when the GMC visitation took place, the idea of a new hospital had become something of a sick joke. The firm recommendation of the visitors was therefore described as a 'bombshell', particularly as it was seen to carry with it the implication that failure to build it could spell the end of the Cork medical school. For the first time, University College Cork began to take an active interest in the matter and the need for a new hospital again came under active consideration.

There was, however, little enough agreement as to where things should go from here. Newer members of the medical faculty campaigned actively for the immediate planning and building of a regional hospital at Wilton; staff members of the voluntary hospitals had reservations about this because of its possible effects on their own hospitals, while both the CEO of the Health Board and the older staff members at St Finbarr's favoured modernising the old hospital instead of building a new one. A further group pressed for the expansion of St Stephen's Hospital at Sarsfield's Court, and its adoption as the 'new' general hospital. Many of the politicians on the Health Board were against Wilton, citing expense and relative satisfaction with the existing state of affairs as reasons, and they voted by a majority against it.

Again the prospect of getting a new hospital seemed lost, but, by 1963, the Department of Health had been persuaded to think otherwise and the minister, Seán MacEntee, refused to accept the decision of the Health Authority. He directed that if they would not build the hospital at Wilton, he would get another authority to build it. Understandably, the Health Board's decision was quickly revoked. After this, matters were further delayed by a suggestion from the Department of Health that an international design competition be held for the planning of the new multimillion pound project. This grandiose scheme wasted further time and came to nothing but, in 1966, was replaced by a ministerial decision to hold a competition to select an architect to design the hospital as well as a new dental hospital and school. Those of us who were convinced of the importance and urgency of building Wilton were near despair. Fortunately, Jack Lynch was now Taoiseach and, with his help, a new order was made in 1967 to empower the newly formed Cork Hospital Board to design and build the hospital and dental school. The board comprised representatives from UCC, the Health Authority and the Department of Health; architects were chosen in 1968, building began in 1972 and the Cork Regional Hospital was opened for patients on 30 November 1978. It was officially opened, appropriately, by Mr Jack Lynch, who was once again Taoiseach, on 7 May 1979.

With 600 beds, all the major specialties except obstetrics (which is now being added), extensive lecturing and teaching with some library and research facilities, it was Ireland's most complete hospital. Its opening marked a new era in clinical medicine and teaching in Cork. The seventeen years of political and medical dissent, endless entreaty with later prolonged and tedious planning caused much frustration, irritation and seemingly endless time and energy consumption to those of us who were deeply and passionately involved. Looking back now, there would seem no doubt that it was worth all the effort and waiting.

Planning and building of the new dental school and hospital continued until its opening in 1982–83. It is a striking and effective replacement of the old dental hospital and school near the North Infirmary where dentistry had been taught since the initiation of the BDS degree in 1913–14.

9

The 1960s and a Changing Medical School

While the building of a new hospital was clearly a major recommendation of the 1961 visitors, it was obvious to even the most optimistic that this would at best take some years and, furthermore, that this alone would not be sufficient to achieve a viable and effective medical school. Many glaring defects and omissions had to be faced at the teaching hospitals and in faculty.

St Finbarr's Hospital had, by now, clearly become the most important teaching hospital and also the one where improvements were most needed and achievable. The visitors' perception of the hospital has already been recorded and it is of interest to learn what the general public thought of it. Patrick Cockburn, the author and press

Medical Professorial Unit, St Finbarr's Hospital, mid-1970s

correspondent, was a young patient there with poliomyelitis in 1956, and in his recently published book *The Broken Boy*[1] states, 'For people in Cork, St Finbarr's still had the whiff of the old poorhouse it had once been, a place offering rude shelter to the destitute and the dying who had nowhere else to go. In the early 1950s most of the wards, though not the one I was in, were still heated by open fires.' While the heating had improved by 1961, the people's perception of the hospital had altered little. This did not seem to greatly worry the majority of the clinical consultants, many of whose interests lay elsewhere, but fortunately the senior administrators of the newly formed Health Board and the Medical Superintendent, Dr Michael Goold, were keen to co-operate in any efforts to improve and modernise the old hospital. Happily, the economic and political climate of the early 1960s was also favourable. Seán Lemass had replaced the ageing and conservative De Valera as Taoiseach and, in the improving economic scene, his maxim that 'a rising tide lifted all ships' held true for government support of projects designed to lift the old but important hospital.

Improvements began in the struggling, new medical professorial unit when a ward complex was created in an area which had in the past housed unmarried mothers and their newborn infants. This, among other benefits, meant that it became possible for the recently appointed professor to care for both male and female in-patients. Some office facilities were provided and, importantly, an area where small-group lectures and clinical demonstrations could be carried out was included.

Gradually, both the staff and facilities at St Finbarr's were developed. An important early addition to the staff was Cork's first geriatric physician. The hospital had large numbers of long-stay elderly patients and the need for modern geriatric care was great. With the appointment of Dr Michael Hyland, this was provided with dramatic and gratifying results. Other medical specialties were also established: neurology, gastro-enterology, cardiology, dermatology, and, later, nephrology and haematology, all developed in the late 1960s and early 1970s, while the appointment of a neurosurgeon preceded other changes associated with the development of a full-time Department of Surgery. Improvement in and expansion of the pathology services at the hospital both preceded and followed the major changes which occurred with the establishment of a new university department there. Later, further radiologists arrived in the dilapidated and cramped old x-ray department. Catering facilities were established to facilitate the staff which was expanding in every sector and finally a new Accident and Emergency Unit was built, and quickly became frantically busy.

In the early years of all these changes, some of the institutions and practices of the old workhouse persisted. Consultants and some other ranks were clocked in and out of the hospital gate daily, ward names such as the 'Male and Female Protestant' persisted, and an ageing workhouse inmate (Duncan) delivered messages on his bicycle while another, driving his horse and 'butt', made his way with vegetables from the hospital fields to the kitchens among ambulances bearing patients to and from complex, modern and sophisticated investigational and therapeutic procedures.

Coinciding with the more obvious improvements and additions in the hospital, more subtle and yet, in some ways, more important changes were taking place in perceptions and attitudes at St Finbarr's. At first, these perhaps coincided with the establishment of a medical professorial unit but the hospital gradually came to see itself as a definitive teaching hospital. Undergraduate students, never unwelcome, now began to perceive themselves as part, indeed an important part, of the hospital entity while nursing staff and others reciprocated by treating them as such. Postgraduate teaching sessions began and were attended not just by non-consultant hospital staff but by junior academic staff from UCC and, equally significantly, by a few family doctors, notably by Dr Owen Shorten whose continued interest and support had a very positive influence on the development of education for and by general practitioners in UCC. Clinical research, though gravely limited by total lack of funding and facilities, began in a small way and even the attitude of the general public to the hospital changed gradually, in that it began to be seen as not just the workhouse but as a hospital where a high standard of acute care was available.

College and Faculty Developments

Quite apart from the struggle to achieve a new teaching hospital and to develop and improve facilities in the old ones in the interim, UCC and its medical faculty had many other problems and challenges to face after the divisive and depressing 1950s and the constructive but, nevertheless, demanding visitation of 1961. Graduate numbers were small and the numbers of Irish nationals graduating in the early 1960s were hardly sufficient to justify the continuation of a Cork medical school in spite of the very cogent arguments for the need for it made by the visitors. Urgent changes and developments were needed in a faculty not renowned for its dynamism, innovation or cohesion.

One individual who was actively supportive was the president, Henry St J. Atkins. He was a Cork city man (the first to become president in the then more than one hundred years of the college), a North Monastery boy and a Cork hurler – yet he had none of the connotations that this combination would suggest. He had a rather quiet disposition, was not a big socialiser and his main interests were in the college and mathematics, in which subject he had been professor. He was registrar of the college during O'Rahilly's presidency and his task in succeeding him was not an easy one. He followed an aggressive polymath, a man who was a national figure as well as a president and who had made an indelible imprint on the nature and perception of the college. In contrast, Harry Atkins was affable, polite and slow to give offence. His critics branded him as weak, inoffensive and ineffectual but he had to preside over a college which was in straitened economic circumstances, whose very existence he needed to preserve and this he did with considerable skill and success. He took a deep and helpful interest in the medical faculty throughout his nine-year presidency (some suggested this was in part because two of his children were medical graduates, but both his predecessor and successor also had offspring who were similarly qualified). In the early years of his tenure, Atkins defended the medical school as best he could against the many damning criticisms of the 1953 and 1954 visitations, while making every effort to comply with their requests. In later years, he was an enthusiastic supporter of the plans for a new teaching hospital and also helped as much as he could the new Department of Medicine. In general, he was a decent, gentle and honourable man whose career as president deserves more praise than it is often accorded.

From 1961, the medical faculty faced its many problems with considerable energy and effect. It addressed the visitors' recommendations regarding St Stephen's and St Mary's Orthopaedic hospitals; in the latter, Mr St John O'Connell was already a faculty member while St Stephen's became a teaching hospital in 1964 with Mr Maurice Hickey being appointed a lecturer in surgery two years later. Discussions also began with Limerick consultants and, in 1966, the Limerick Regional became a teaching hospital, soon followed by the maternity and orthopaedic hospitals in Limerick and Croom. Even though it received little enough publicity at the time, the inclusion of a medical complex outside of Cork as part of the school was a very significant step in the evolution of undergraduate medical education in Munster. In retrospect, more could have been done to integrate more fully the two centres but, nevertheless, it was a very worthwhile beginning.

Departmental Developments and Appointments

Pathology was one of the subjects most criticised in the 1961 and previous visitations. Clearly, the department needed root-and-branch reform and this did not prove easy. Clinical biochemistry was first declared a teaching subject and the new appointee at St Finbarr's, together with the consultant bacteriologist Dr B. V. Foley became staff members of the evolving department. With the retirement of Professor William O'Donovan, a new full-time appointment was established. Professor Colin Wright, a Yorkshireman who had been senior lecturer at Leeds University, was appointed professor with a joint appointment similar to that of medicine. Full spatial integration of the department did not, however, prove possible until the Regional Hospital opened.

When Professor Kiely retired from the chair of surgery in 1967, he was replaced by Professor Michael P. Brady in a further full-time professorship. Professor Brady, a UCD graduate and a Dubliner who had trained chiefly in St Vincent's Hospital in Dublin and in Boston, was young and dynamic and played a very significant role in the development of the school. He created an excellent academic department at St Finbarr's, was himself a much respected surgeon with special interests in vascular and endocrine diseases and also was deeply interested in faculty development and wider aspects of medical education both under- and postgraduate.

Psychiatry and paediatrics were the next full-time departments to be established, though this did not prove possible until the 1970s. Psychiatry had historically been located in the Cork Mental (later Our Lady's) Hospital but it was decided to change all of this and develop a new university department at St Stephen's Hospital, where, with the marked decline in tuberculosis, beds had become available. The development was long overdue and was beneficial to both the clinical and academic aspects of the subject. The new (and first) Professor of Psychiatry was Robert J. Daly, a Trinity graduate, English-born of Cork origins with extensive academic and clinical experience in Britain and the USA. The unit was successful and innovative, it served the patients of the South Lee area and maintained close links with both the community and other academic departments. With the opening of the Regional Hospital, the psychiatric unit moved to Wilton where it continues.

The position of paediatrics both as an academic subject and as a service to the community in Cork had long been anomalous, not to say farcical. Dr Richard G. G. Barry, a native of Carrigtwohill and a UCC graduate of the mid-1930s who learned his paediatrics in England, was appointed a temporary physician with responsibility for paediatrics at St Finbarr's Hospital (then the Cork District Hospital) in 1949. The post was temporary with a contract for six months, renewable at the discretion of the authority, and so it remained for the next twenty years. Dr Barry was Cork's first, and for some years its only, paediatrician. The medical faculty recognised him as a teacher in paediatrics in 1951 and he was appointed a part-time lecturer in the late 1950s. It was not until 1969 that it became possible to create a full-time Department of Paediatrics. The post was advertised and, after interview, Dick Barry was appointed professor. By then, of course, he was in his late fifties and held the chair until his retirement in 1978. He was a fine clinician and teacher, a phenomenally hard worker and his contribution to paediatrics in Cork was immense.

Thus with the exception of obstetrics and gynaecology, fundamental changes took place in all the 'major' clinical subjects during the 1960s and early 1970s. In 1977, when Professor William Kearney retired from the part-time chair in obstetrics and gynaecology in which he had been successful and popular for twenty-nine years, the final full-time clinical department was established. Professor David Jenkins, a Welshman who had graduated from Queen's University Belfast and who gained his postgraduate experience there and in Leeds, was appointed a year later with full-time duties in the Erinville Maternity and in the regional hospitals.

Full-time clinical lectureships in the new departments followed. All of the appointees were independent clinical consultants in the hospitals to which they were appointed. A number of other new consultant posts in different specialties were also created, mainly at St Finbarr's which, by the time the Regional Hospital opened, almost had the staff if not the buildings and facilities of a modern teaching hospital.

In the so-called 'minor' clinical subjects, changes were taking place as well. When Professor O'Hea-Cussen retired, ophthalmology and otorhinolaryngology were separated and recognised clinical teachers were appointed in each as parts of the departments of medicine and surgery respectively. In the public health area, the emphasis gradually moved towards social medicine and the department was at first called 'Social and Preventive Medicine' and finally 'Social Medicine'. Dr John P. Corridan was appointed the first Professor of Social Medicine in 1973. He had worked in the public health department at Cork City Hall but, during the 1960s, had become increasingly interested in medicine in the elderly and in the teaching of family medicine to undergraduates. Pharmacology, where Dr D. P. O'Mahony was full-time lecturer, absorbed pharmacy while therapeutics, where Dr O. T. D. Loughnan had been part-time lecturer since the 1940s, became increasingly associated with medicine. Forensic and social medicine became closely linked as did anaesthesia and surgery. None of these changes were of fundamental significance but reflected more the medical educational thinking of the time.

The Pre-Clinical Subjects

While the visitors of both the mid-1950s and of 1961 found that the pre-clinical departments were understaffed and overworked, their overall opinions of the standard and competence of the subjects were not unfavourable. Professor MacConaill, while flamboyant in manner, was both competent and hardworking, serving his subject and faculty well during his thirty-one years in the chair of anatomy. In physiology, Professor Frank Kane returned to Dublin in 1954 after a somewhat uneventful twelve years in Cork and was replaced by another Dubliner, Paul Cannon, whose stay in Cork was brief; he moved back to UCD but retained a friendly and helpful interest in his old department. During Cannon's tenure of office, he was joined by Dr John D. Sheehan who became lecturer and then professor. Professor Sheehan trained and qualified as a physician with a special interest in respiratory diseases and served as a consultant in Africa for a brief time before returning to Cork (where he had qualified in 1948). His clinical training and interests proved a great asset to the development of physiology in Cork. He was firm and uncompromising yet scrupulously fair with students. In medical faculty and other committees, he was forthright and trenchant but his contribution to the medical school was immense, and he was one of the hardest and most effective workers in the advancement of medicine at UCC over three decades. He and MacConaill were strikingly different in personality and work methods and yet were a curiously satisfactory combination.

Biochemistry, a critically important subject in medicine, never seemed to become deeply involved in faculty affairs. Professor Tom Brady was not a medical graduate and, while he provided an efficient and co-operative service in the teaching of medical undergraduates, his interests, both research and political, were always more closely associated with the science faculty in which biochemistry was an important and influential unit. During the 1960s and 1970s, it grew quite markedly in size and importance and yet, when clinical biochemistry became a more recognised academic subject, it was decided that it should become part of the Department of Medicine rather than of biochemistry. Thus biochemistry, while contributing much to undergraduate medical education, was in many ways somewhat detached from more general medical faculty developments.

Students and Graduates

While the medical faculty was undergoing great changes during the 1960s, student and graduate patterns were altering too. Cork had always been a small school and, apart from the 1940s, graduate numbers rarely exceeded fifty per year. In the 1950s, numbers fell quite markedly in spite of the addition of Americans and others. In 1962, there were only twelve graduates, nine of whom were Irish and one female (Ann Wall). This was the smallest number for thirty years – in 1932 only eleven qualified – and one of the smallest of the century. Once again, fears were expressed about the viability of such a small school with renewed suggestions that all medical undergraduate teaching might be centralised in Dublin. Happily, however, numbers began to increase and, by the end of the decade, class sizes had increased to fifty. In fact by the mid- to late 1960s, the pre-clinical members of faculty began to worry about the ability of the school's current staff to teach the increasing numbers. The clinical members, on the other hand, favoured the expansion of student numbers as they were keen that Cork, with its adequate number of teaching beds and relative plenitude of clinical teachers, should be seen as a viable medical school. There were many discussions at faculty meetings regarding the optimal number of undergraduate medical students and how this might be controlled. Eventually, the concept of an agreed number of entries, with selection largely based on Leaving Certificate results, with allowances being made for a limited number of mature students and overseas graduates, was adopted, and has persisted over the years in spite of marked changes in the numbers of admissions and the proportion of non-Irish (later non-EU) entrants. Other criteria for admission to medicine, such as selection of a proportion by interview and a common First Science examination, were tried but discarded as being less effective or fair. Faculty has, over the years, recognised the weaknesses and disadvantages of depending on the results of a single examination for entry to medicine but has consistently felt that the system was effective and just. The arguments for and against the arrangement persist and are likely to continue to do so.

An unexpected change in the 1960s was in the destination of graduates, where they settled permanently in their careers. From the founding of the school, a majority of graduates emigrated, chiefly to Britain as family doctors but, during the twentieth century, to a variety of other places as well. During the 1960s and in subsequent decades, however, the largest proportion settled in Ireland. Their reasons for doing so were probably multiple; more job opportunities and an improved economy at home combined with more optimism and confidence in the Irish health services were probably the most cogent reasons for their decisions.

Those graduates of the 1960s who either remained in Ireland or returned there after postgraduate training abroad, did so in a variety of specialties but the majority were general practitioners. Family medicine was expanding and thriving in Ireland in the 1970s when the greatest proportion settled permanently here, and Cork graduates were among the most active members of the College of General Practitioners and other organisations promoting improvements of clinical standards. The high-class patient care they provided was widely appreciated and improved the image of the school both locally and nationally. The charge that Cork was a college that trained doctors for export had often been levelled at the medical faculty by its critics and it was comforting for faculty members that this perception was no longer valid.

Not everyone, it would seem, shared these positive attitudes to the school and its students. Professor John A. Murphy in his detailed, but (in the opinion of this author) not always unbiased history *The College*,[2] from which I have derived much information regarding the early years of QCC/UCC, had this to say of the students of the early 1960s: 'Medical students (male) had a swaggering self-confidence based on a cocky view of their own importance in Cork society which entitled them to range freely in the pastures of sex and drink. Coolly disregarding authoritarianism, convinced of their own superiority, and indeed by the snobbery and inferiority complex of other students, they dominated, one might say overbalanced, college society.' As one who, unlike Murphy, held a senior position in faculty and academic council for much of this time and knew the medical students well, I can only say that I profoundly disagree with these views.

10

A Decade of Achievement into the 1970s

While great energy went into planning and legis-
lating for change in the 1960s, the results of these
efforts were mainly achieved during the 1970s.
They were greatly aided by the enthusiasm and
persistence of the then president, Michael Donal
McCarthy, who had been appointed in 1967 in
succession to Professor John J. McHenry. The latter,
a physicist, was president for only three years as he
was in his late sixties when appointed. While he
was efficient, he had neither the time nor the incli-
nation for achieving major change. McCarthy on
the other hand, had worked in UCC in the 1940s
when he was Professor of Mathematical Physics,
before moving to Dublin to become assistant
director and then director of the Central Statistics

Office. On returning to Cork, his highly intelligent and analytical mind quickly saw the imperfections and anachronisms of the college and he set about righting these without delay. He quickly appreciated the efforts which were being made to improve matters in medicine and was a valuable and powerful influence for good, both within the college and in dealings with the Department of Health and the Cork Health Authority. His overall achievements in office were outstanding and he was one of the greatest presidents. Where Windle transformed the college at the turn of the twentieth century, fifty years later, McCarthy converted UCC from an outdated and inefficient institution to a modern college.

In faculty itself, although the major developments were in the clinical areas, significant changes also took place in anatomy and physiology. When Michael MacConaill retired in 1973 he was replaced by Gerald N. C. Crawford who had been a lecturer in anatomy at Oxford and a Fellow of Magdalen College before his appointment. He never really settled in Cork and resigned his chair after only four years, moving to Sheffield University in 1977. Fortunately for the medical school, Dr John D. Fraher, a UCC graduate of 1966 who had extensive postgraduate training in Britain before returning to Cork as lecturer, was available for the chair which he has occupied since with distinction. His artistic knowledge and skills together with his undoubted anatomical ability have made him a sought-after and gifted lecturer in the area of anatomical art. At a more mundane level, he has made many advances in the area of the neurosciences and has built up the largest Department of Anatomy in Ireland. Recently, he has been deeply involved in the founding and development of the BioSciences Institute in UCC. This is the first interdisciplinary, purpose-built, research unit in the biosciences in this country and is an exciting new challenge.

In physiology, Professor Sheehan carried a heavy load in his earlier years as professor and the appointment of Dr John W. Hall as lecturer in 1965 must have been a very welcome development for him. John Hall graduated in 1960 and did much of his postgraduate training in Sheffield where he carried out valuable research in prostaglandin metabolism. His success as a lecturer in Cork led to his being appointed associate professor in 1976 and he succeeded Professor Sheehan on his retirement in the mid-1980s. Apart from his many contributions to physiology, Professor Hall was a greatly valued and innovative faculty dean in the 1990s before his retirement at the turn of the twenty-first century.

Full-time clinical lectureships were established and filled in all the major departments. In pathology, Professor Wright, after a somewhat difficult time in Cork, resigned his chair and returned to Britain. He was replaced by the then full-time lecturer, Dr Cuimín

Doyle, an Offaly man and UCD graduate whose postgraduate training had been in Glasgow and Dublin. He had, on appointment, the difficult undertaking of organising a new department in the newly opened Regional Hospital. This he carried out with great efficiency but one of the highlights of his early days as professor was his management of the pathological problems posed by the Air India disaster which took place off the coast of West Cork in the summer of 1985. Following the explosion and plane crash, the remains of 132 passengers were recovered and brought ashore to the Cork Regional Hospital. Here, the complex and extremely difficult tasks of identification, forensic investigation and post-mortem examination had to be carried out while 450 relatives of the deceased (mostly Indian and Canadian) were interviewed, counselled and helped. This was accomplished with complete success and reflected huge credit on Professor Doyle and his colleagues as well as on Dr Mick Molloy who provided the clinical backup.

During the 1970s, student and graduate numbers continued to grow. By this time, the two were closely linked as those students who began the study of medicine usually completed it, in marked contrast to what had happened in the first one hundred years of the college. The change may have been due in part to the selection of students for medicine and to an altered economic climate but the introduction of the 'two-year rule' was undoubtedly an important factor. This excluded from further study of medicine those students who had failed their examination on four successive occasions (exams being taken twice in each year). While not many were actually excluded from medicine by the rule, its presence and the fear of exclusion which it generated had a salutary effect on student scholastic efforts. In any case, the numbers graduating rose from fifty a year at the beginning of the decade to seventy at its end. There was much demand for entry into medicine but numbers were limited by both college and national rulings. From about 1970, the proportion of women studying medicine began to increase and this gender change continued and increased further in the next two decades. This and other matters concerning women in medicine will be considered in detail below (pp. 97–102).

Like those of the previous decade, the graduates of the 1970s settled in Ireland in greater numbers than elsewhere. Again, general practice was their most popular choice. After Ireland, Britain continued to be the next most favoured place of permanent employment. In contrast to earlier years, however, increasing numbers of Cork graduates became hospital consultants throughout England and Wales, while those who chose family medicine tended to do so in more salubrious areas, an indication perhaps of the increased esteem in which they had begun to be held.

The decade ended with two notable retirements: Professor Dick Barry from paediatrics and Dr Donal McCarthy from the presidency. Both had given unstinting and immensely valuable service to the college and to medical faculty and were greatly missed.

The Regional Hospital Opens

The opening of the Regional Hospital on 30 November 1978 was not only a historic event but also probably unique in the manner in which it happened. It consisted of a transfer of patients and staff of all descriptions from St Finbarr's Hospital directly to Wilton (some three miles away on the other side of the city) over a period of two days. In all, more than 200 patients were transferred from the acute wards of St Finbarr's, most of them on the 30 November. The event was planned with great precision. Patients breakfasted and had their appropriate treatment in the morning at St Finbarr's and were then transferred by a fleet of ambulances and CIÉ buses to Wilton where they were frequently met by the very doctors, nurses and attendants who had looked after

Cork Regional Hospital, 1978

Welcoming the first patient to Cork Regional Hospital, 30 November 1978. (left to right) Sr. M. Thecla, matron; Emily Curren (in wheelchair), first patient; Mr. Tony Fitzgerald, wheelchair attendant; Mr. Michael Cogan, head porter

them earlier that day. Not a single hitch occurred in the whole procedure which was carried out with great good humour and some hilarity.

The local press quickly named the new hospital 'The Wilton Hilton', perceiving the wards and other facilities as the height of luxury. In fact, from the strictly medical point of view, it was (and remains) Ireland's most complete hospital and its 600 beds embrace a fuller range of specialties than any other. With the transfer of ophthalmology there when the Eye, Ear and Throat Hospital closed in the late 1980s and now the imminent opening of a major obstetric unit replacing the services of at least both the Erinville and St Finbarr's, it has become an even more comprehensive medical centre.

From the teaching and research points of view, its opening brought many benefits. Lecture theatres meant that a majority of didactic lectures could be given on site.

Teaching rooms on each floor greatly facilitated clinical instruction (although they have been gradually 'stolen' to accommodate increasing clinical needs). A comprehensive Department of Pathology enabled the university department to, at last, find a home in a teaching hospital as the 1961 visitors had so earnestly demanded. A dedicated research area was built adjoining pathology but it soon became too small to cope with growing research needs and was substantially added to in the early 1990s when the Department of Clinical Pharmacology was built and the Department of Medicine expanded.

While bricks and mortar never built a good medical school, the opening of the Regional Hospital was profoundly beneficial to Cork. The work that had gone into creating, staffing and improving clinical departments at St Finbarr's was, in part, made possible and certainly expedited by the perceived need to have them ready for the new hospital. Similarly, the reasons put forward for the establishment of new and much needed consultant posts often included the argument that such posts would be required in a new 600-bed teaching hospital. Consultant staff numbers were, in fact, greatly increased in and around the time of the opening of the Regional but these were badly needed anyway in what had been up to then a grossly understaffed teaching hospital service.

As far as undergraduate students were concerned, the new hospital had multiple advantages. Bedside and lecture teaching facilities were available conveniently and close together, library and reading facilities were on hand as never before and new specialties and teachers provided more comprehensive clinical education. The changes which began soon after in the voluntary hospitals further helped to provide both undergraduate and postgraduate students with education facilities hitherto only dreamt of.

In passing, tribute must be paid to St Finbarr's Hospital which assumed a new clinical and a greatly diminished teaching role at this time. During most of the 1960s and 1970s, it played a major and critical part in the changes in clinical and academic medicine which were taking place. The ageing, old-fashioned former workhouse adapted itself to and coped with these changes with an efficiency, good humour and grace that almost defies description. Everyone who worked there looks back on the exciting times and remarkable achievements with wonder and gratitude and to many (including this author) those years at St Finbarr's were the best and happiest of their careers.

The Voluntary Hospitals

While the major improvements at St Finbarr's and the opening of the Regional Hospital greatly benefited both the general public and the medical school, the situation in the Cork voluntary general hospitals was far from satisfactory. The North and South infirmaries were among the oldest hospitals in the country and were the original teaching hospitals in Cork – medicine had been taught in them long before the college medical school was established. The Mercy and Victoria hospitals dated from the middle of the nineteenth century and, while their status as teaching hospitals could not compare with the infirmaries, they had provided a valuable service to the people of south Munster. With the development of St Finbarr's Hospital in the mid-twentieth century, the importance of the voluntary hospitals from both the academic and clinical points of view, lessened considerably. They were comparatively small in size and each hospital maintained its independence from the others. Sub-specialty development did not take place at a time when this was becoming essential and, furthermore, their systems of appointing consultants, while improving, was not always above reproach. They perceived themselves – probably with some justification – as receiving less favoured treatment from the Department of Health and UCC than the other hospitals. There was talk at central level of their ultimate replacement by a second large general hospital and while nobody in Cork really believed that this would happen in the foreseeable future, their outlook, in the form they were in, looked far from promising.

In the mid-1970s, it was timely, therefore, that serious consideration began to be given to some form of amalgamation and rationalisation of their services and, in 1977, the four public voluntary hospitals in the city were federated under the Cork Voluntary Hospitals Board, with the objective of their ultimate amalgamation into one new hospital. The board was made up of representatives of each of the hospitals and addressed the interests and problems common to all of them. Thus, much duplication was avoided, a number of joint consultant appointments were made and all of the participating hospitals were able to function more efficiently. The board was also able to discuss overall medical problems in the Cork area with the Southern Health Board and the Department of Health, to the advantage of all parties.

Although it functioned actively for less than a decade, being overtaken somewhat by other events and advances, the Voluntary Hospitals Board was undoubtedly beneficial to both the individual hospitals and to medicine in Cork. While, at first, it was viewed by some as a rival to the Health Board complex of hospitals, in fact the two groups worked well and productively together and it paved the way for greater co-ordination and rationalisation of Cork's hospital services. The different hospitals in the group evolved and fared very differently in the years following the board's establishment and what befell each of them merits individual consideration.

The Mercy Hospital

The Mercy is the largest of the voluntary hospitals. It was founded in 1857 in the former Mansion House, which had been built by the celebrated architect Ducrot in 1757. The city authorities gave the house to the Sisters of Mercy (as they felt that it was too large and expensive to maintain as a mayoral residence), who converted it to a forty-bed hospital at a cost of £3,793. By 1893, there were eighty beds and a further sixty were added in 1917. While it was designated a teaching hospital and had no fewer than eight professors on its staff over the years, little enough teaching was carried out there and it was subjected to criticism by the GMC visitation of 1954 and its teaching status was withdrawn. By the 1960s, it had 230 beds but no outpatient facilities. During that decade, however, a hospital board was established (up to then it had been run solely by the Sisters of Mercy), outpatient sessions were begun and it was again recognised as a teaching hospital in 1966. At that time, the matron stated to medical faculty that 106 public beds were available for teaching (it had a large private sector) and that the Order had agreed that consultant appointments would be made by a board with members nominated equally by medical faculty and the Mercy Sisters with the Catholic bishop or his nominee as chairman. This was a significant advance in Cork medical education and, since then, the hospital has played a valuable role in undergraduate and post-graduate teaching.

Expansion and improvement in specialties, beds and facilities have continued and the Mercy is now a major teaching hospital with 354 beds, a full range of outpatient and inpatient facilities and an internationally acclaimed research programme. In acknowledging its remarkable metamorphosis over the past thirty years, the continued efforts of two people, Dr Michael Bennett and Sister De Pazzi (matron), have to be acclaimed.

The South Infirmary/Victoria Hospital

In spite of its being one of the two original hospitals where medicine was taught in Cork, the origins of the South Infirmary are largely obscure. M. V. Conlon (1943) records: 'By an Act of 1765 the County Infirmary was established in Mallow and the clergy of the Protestant Church created a perpetual corporation for the erection of such Infirmaries. The South Infirmary had been opened in 1762 but was not incorporated until 1771.'[1] By then, it would seem to have been operating as a busy hospital. Efforts were made about 1830 to unite the North and South infirmaries but they were not successful. In

The South Infirmary in the early 1980s.

1861, the County Infirmary in Mallow was moved to Cork and merged with the South Infirmary as the South Charitable Infirmary and County Hospital on a new site close by with fifty-one beds. For the next twenty-three years, the old site was used as a military barracks. After this, the hospital continued to grow in size and importance.

Dr John Woodroffe, already mentioned in regard to his associations with three of the earlier Cork schools and his remarkable abilities in the teaching of anatomy to art students, was a surgeon to the South Infirmary for nearly fifty years (1811–1859). He was very highly regarded by all and it seems strange that he was not more closely associated with Queen's College, which used the South Infirmary as one of its main teaching hospitals from the beginning. There were, however, many notable college teachers on its staff through the years, including two professors of both medicine and surgery and all the professors of obstetrics and gynaecology until the retirement of Professor William Kearney in 1972.

The Victoria Hospital opened as the County and City of Cork Hospital for Women and Children in 1874; one of its founders was the ubiquitous Macnaughton-Jones. It began as a small hospital in Union Quay, then moved to Pope's Quay and, in 1885, found its permanent home in the old South Infirmary buildings. In 1901, on the death of Queen Victoria, the name of the hospital was changed to The Victoria Hospital for Women and Children. It was extensively rebuilt and, after World War II, functioned as a general hospital for a number of years. Both it and its neighbour, the South Infirmary, were slow to modernise and, in time, the logic for their amalgamation became clear. This took place on 1 January 1988.

The combined hospital now has 184 inpatient beds and a day unit with twenty beds. It has been greatly developed and is a busy teaching hospital with a number of specialised departments, as well as several joint appointments with the other teaching hospitals.

The North Infirmary

The North Infirmary, the oldest of the voluntary hospital group, was the first general hospital to be built in Cork. On the outside of the infirmary was the inscription:

Nosocomium
Hoc Deo Auspice
Fundatium
Anno Salutis
1720

In 1829, Revd Dr Quarry, the then chairman, stated, 'The North Infirmary was erected in 1720. It is the most ancient provincial hospital in the Empire.'[2] It was built in the grounds of an even older medical institution, the Chamber of Medicines and Physic Garden. For lack of funds, it was unable to admit patients until 1744 when it was staffed by eleven physicians and five surgeons of the city who visited the infirmary in their turn and gave their services for free. By 1750, it became possible to appoint two physicians and a surgeon at a fixed salary of £20 per annum (the apothecary was paid £30 per annum). Some twenty years later, the principal physician was Dr Robert Emmet, father of the patriot of the same name. Dr Emmet left Cork in 1770 to take up the post of State Physician in Dublin, a post which he held until 1803, the year of his son's rebellion, trial for treason and subsequent execution.

The North Infirmary continued as a general hospital until 1988 and had many distinguished staff members through the years, including four professors of surgery and one of medicine. Its relatively small size (103 beds) and comparative lack of specialisation made it increasingly vulnerable, but nevertheless the announcement (at government

The North Infirmary in the early 1980s

level) that it was to close came as a great surprise. This happened at a time when the national economy was in deep trouble and when there were many swingeing health cuts. While the North Infirmary up to the time of its closure played a useful role in serving the citizens of the north side of the city, its survival was probably made less likely by its comparative closeness to the then rapidly developing and expanding Mercy Hospital. Nevertheless, it seems a pity that an institution with such a venerable history and one which was held in affectionate esteem locally, could not have been retained for some medical purpose – perhaps as a centre for family medicine – which would continue to benefit the people of the Shandon area.

Thus, by the end of the 1980s, there were three general teaching hospitals in Cork and also three specialised hospitals where ophthalmology with otorhinolaryngology, obstetrics and psychiatry had been taught for many years. Their separate stories are also worth recounting.

11

The Specialist Teaching Hospitals

The Eye, Ear and Throat Hospital

Another teaching hospital to close in the late 1980s was the Eye, Ear and Throat Hospital. The original hospital was founded in Nile Street (now Sheares' Street) in 1868 by the indefatigable Henry Macnaughton-Jones who, among his many appointments, was its first physician. The hospital on the Western Road was opened in 1897, its building was organised by Arthur W. Sandford, another colourful character who has already been described. His long regime there was followed by another of even greater length, that of Vernon O'Hea-Cussen. Following his retirement, ophthalmology and ENT became separate subjects academically. When the hospital was closed by order of the Minister of Health in 1988 (the same year as the North Infirmary closure), ophthalmology services were transferred to the Regional Hospital and ear, nose and throat surgery to the South Infirmary/Victoria Hospital. The building currently houses the Health Promotion Unit of the Health Service Executive.

The Erinville and St Finbarr's Maternity Hospitals

The only major clinical subject in which there was no change in clinical location or emphasis during the 1960s and most of the 1970s was obstetrics and gynaecology. Obstetrics was practised and taught in the Erinville and St Finbarr's hospitals with the then professor, William Kearney, in the Erinville and Dr Reginald C. Sutton, one of the part-time lecturers, in charge at St Finbarr's.

The Erinville Hospital was opened in 1898, replacing the Lying-In Hospital in Nile Street where the first Professor of Midwifery, Joshua Reuben Harvey, taught. Macnaughton-Jones was co-founder of the Cork Maternity Hospital – at first also in Nile Street but later in nearby Bachelor's Quay – where he taught, as did his successor, Professor Henry Corby. Both of these earlier hospitals were small and situated in the Marsh area where many of the poorest in Cork then lived. The Erinville was originally named the County and City of Cork Lying-In Hospital. It was added to gradually and, when the Cork Maternity Hospital closed in 1928, became much busier. By the 1950s, the number of deliveries had increased greatly and a further enlarged hospital now has more than 3,000 deliveries annually.

Obstetrics and gynaecology had been practised in what is now St Finbarr's Hospital since the workhouse was opened in 1840. The opening of a new Maternity Hospital of fifty-one beds on the site in 1952 (the first major post-war hospital building) made a major difference to the Cork obstetric scene. It has more than 2,000 deliveries annually and, with the Erinville, provides almost all the public maternity services in Cork city and county as well as the clinical medical and nursing training.

The markedly increased workload at the Erinville and St Finbarr's was associated with (and perhaps the result of) major change in the pattern of obstetric care which took place in Cork and elsewhere about the middle of the twentieth century. Until then many of the lower-income group and some of the middle- and upper-income earners had their babies at home, tended by midwives with supervision by the family or other doctor when necessary. A large number of women from the middle- and upper-income groups had their deliveries in nursing homes, of which there were many in cities like Cork. A significant proportion of the deliveries which took place in hospital were the

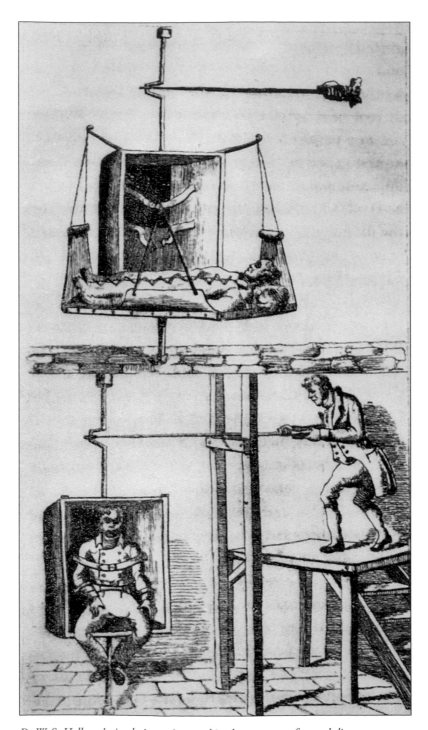

Dr W. S. Halloran's circulating swing, used in the treatment of mental disease

complex and abnormal ones. At about the middle of the century, however, hospital deliveries became much more frequent and soon came to be considered the norm. The value to both mother and baby of hospital facilities with specialist obstetricians and paediatricians became widely recognised and happily this state of affairs persists. It, inevitably, led to greatly increased demand for both maternity hospitals and consultant obstetricians. The number of hospital deliveries increased greatly and both the Erinville and St Finbarr's are nearly always full to capacity.

Professor David Jenkins, Cork's first full-time Professor of Obstetrics and Gynaecology retired on 31 January 2000, after a successful term in office during which new academic structures were put in place. He was succeeded by Professor John Higgins. It is now planned that both the teaching hospitals will be replaced by a single large unit which has been built as part of the now Cork University Hospital. The unit will be state-of-the-art and will open in 2007. It should revolutionise obstetric and gynaecological practice, education and research and is eagerly awaited by all.

Psychiatry in Cork

The hospital treatment of psychiatric disease in Cork appears to have begun with the establishment of the Cork Lunatic Asylum in 1791. This was situated close to the House of Industry, near the Victoria Hospital and is best remembered for its first Medical Superintendent, Dr William Saunders Halloran. He was an able and benevolent man and is stated to have been 'the first physician to advocate and carry out the humane treatment of lunatics'.[1] Although he held office well before the Queen's College medical school was established, he is worthy of mention as one of Cork's most inventive and distinguished psychiatrists, who employed many treatments in mental disease. These included bleeding, emetics, purgatives, opium, camphor, blistering, mercury baths and, not least, the circulating swing which appears to have been his own invention. This worked like a windlass and could be revolved at rates of up to a hundred times per minute, being regulated to the degree best suited to the individual patient. It also included a rocking hammock so that the patient could be either rocked quietly to sleep or violently shaken until the necessary purgative or emetic effect was obtained. Thus, it could be used both in mania and depression. In spite of what now seem incongruous treatments, Halloran was a humane and thoughtful man, held in high esteem and regarded, to a degree, as the father of Cork psychiatry.

The Lunatic Asylum was replaced by a large mental hospital, the Eglinton Asylum, built on the Lee Road by the Board of Works with labour provided through a work relief scheme following the Great Famine. It was opened in 1852 and some of the original neo-gothic buildings remain a landmark on the western approaches to Cork city. Transfer of patients from the old asylum took place, but in a rather different way from the next major relocation of patients from Douglas Road to Wilton 126 years later. In the first place, the operation took two months, not two days. Patients are said to have been walked from the Old Blackrock Road to the Lee Road in military fashion between 2.00 a.m. and 4.00 a.m.[2] The timing was probably chosen to avoid their being noticed by or disturbing the Cork citizens of the time.

Psychiatry was taught in the new mental hospital but not until 1881. Up to then, there had been a reluctance to teach the subject at all and it took the concerted efforts of the then Resident Medical Superintendent, Dr James Eames and the president, Dr W. K. Sullivan to persuade the Board of Governors to allow teaching. When it was approved, it had to take place only in the ballroom of the central block of the hospital with students not allowed through the asylum. Dr Eames was appointed lecturer in psychological medicine. Successive superintendents held the lectureship, the title of which was changed to lecturer in mental disease in 1909. One of the best known of these was Dr Bernard F. ('Barney') Honan who held the post from 1933 until 1961, after which he was dean (for a year) and then secretary to medical faculty during some very formative years in the 1960s. The last combined lecturer and medical superintendent was Dr Robert McCarthy. He had some very progressive ideas about downsizing large mental institutions and succeeded in changing the asylum, by then known as Our Lady's Hospital, into a modern 110-bed psychiatric hospital catering for patients from a limited and well-defined catchment area and co-operating fully with the two other major units in the county.

With the establishment of the professorship of psychiatry in 1969 and the appointment of Professor R. J. Daly to St Stephen's Hospital, this latter became the main centre for undergraduate teaching until the unit in the Regional Hospital was opened. Our Lady's Hospital continues as an active psychiatric unit but much of the thirty-seven-acre site (which comprised the original Eglinton Asylum) has been sold for high-end residential building.

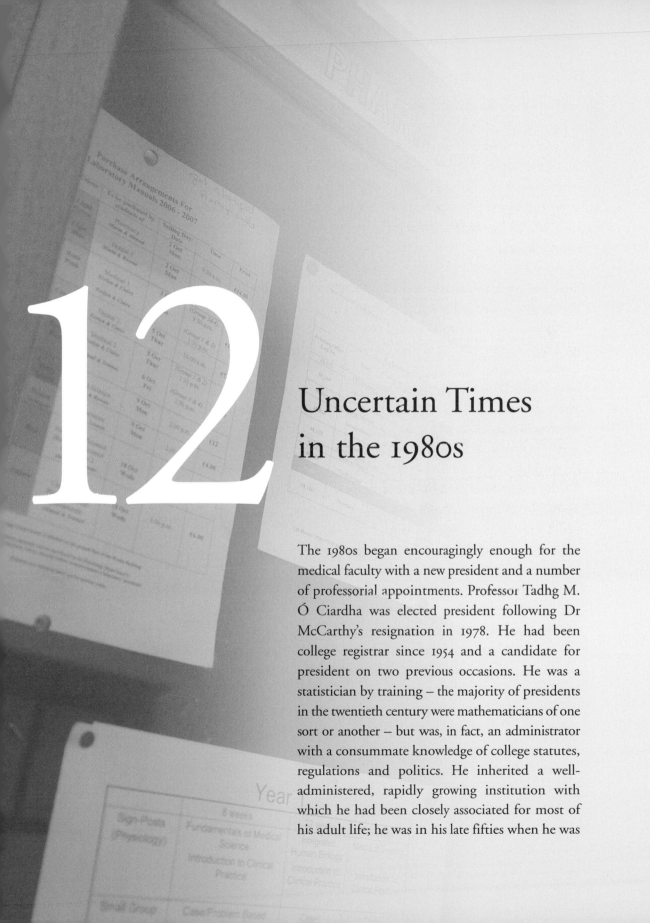

12 Uncertain Times in the 1980s

The 1980s began encouragingly enough for the medical faculty with a new president and a number of professorial appointments. Professor Tadhg M. Ó Ciardha was elected president following Dr McCarthy's resignation in 1978. He had been college registrar since 1954 and a candidate for president on two previous occasions. He was a statistician by training – the majority of presidents in the twentieth century were mathematicians of one sort or another – but was, in fact, an administrator with a consummate knowledge of college statutes, regulations and politics. He inherited a well-administered, rapidly growing institution with which he had been closely associated for most of his adult life; he was in his late fifties when he was appointed president. He was not by nature an innovator but continued with existing developments and enthusiastically supported further growth in a rapidly expanding college. His attitude to medicine in college was fairly neutral. By the time of his appointment, the faculty of medicine, though numerically small relative to total student numbers, had come to be regarded as successful and, by some, as elitist and expensive. While never openly subscribing to these views, Ó Ciardha was not unaware of them and, in the difficult economic times of the late 1980s, was not especially supportive of medicine. An outgoing, sincere and popular character, his overall handling of UCC in a period of rapid expansion and limited resources was effective, if not inspired.

Following Professor Dick Barry's retirement in 1979, two new professors were appointed in the Department of Paediatrics. Dr Peter Kearney became Professor of Paediatrics and Dr Gerald Cussen, Associate Professor of Neonatology. Both were UCC graduates of the 1960s and 1950s respectively; Dr Kearney had worked extensively in Britain and later in Limerick while Dr Cussen had largely trained in Dublin and Canada. Both had beds in the Regional Hospital while Dr Cussen continued his neonatal work at the Erinville Hospital where he had worked as a lecturer. Further associate chairs were established: Dr J. B. Ferriss in medicine, Mr Liam Kirwan in surgery and later Dr P. F. Duggan in clinical chemistry (in the Department of Medicine).

An important advance in the involvement of the staffs of the teaching hospitals in faculty affairs, was the creation of a number of places on the faculty board for representatives nominated by the staffs of the hospitals, with each nominee serving on the board for a three-year period.

Numbers of students and graduates continued to increase with intense competition among Irish students for the limited number of places available to them. During this time, there was a new development in UCC (as well as in the other NUI medical schools) when a policy of taking non-European students was adopted. They were mostly from Middle and Far East countries and they paid far higher fees than their Irish counterparts. While they brought welcome funds to college, the additional numbers placed added strains on already overworked and understaffed departments, who hoped that the money accruing would, at least in part, go to help their financially straitened faculty but were unable to ascertain if any or how much of it did so. College administration firmly maintained that such details were matters for the finance committee of the governing body and not for medical faculty. This lack of information combined with the realisation that foreign students were being accepted in a situation where many well-qualified Irish students could not gain admission led to considerable controversy and disquiet. The practice of admitting overseas students into medicine has continued and remains controversial as places for native aspirants become ever more competitive and difficult to attain.

There were a number of other instances where relationships between college administration and medical faculty (either as a whole or in some instances involving individual departments) were somewhat fraught. An example of this was in regard to the teaching of therapeutics when Dr O. T. D. Loughnan retired from the part-time lectureship in 1980 (a post in which he had given sterling service since 1946). Instead of making efforts to fill the post or create a new department, the college authorities merely asked the Department of Medicine to teach the subject without giving an already overstretched unit any help to do so, or even indicating how long this situation might last. In fact, no change was made until the creation of a new Department of Clinical Pharmacology, with the appointment of Professor Michael B. Murphy as its head, in the early 1990s. The importance of the subject can be appreciated from the development and expansion of the department since then. It beggars belief that it was virtually ignored by the college for years while many important advances were taking place elsewhere.

It was, in some ways, understandable that relationships between administration in UCC and the medical faculty should run into difficulties during the 1980s. For much of the decade, the national economy was in a perilous state and overall state finances were straitened. At the same time, third-level education was expanding and, in UCC, growth was rapid and resources limited. Medical student numbers increased somewhat – some of this was due to taking overseas students as the number of Irish was strictly limited – while in other faculties numbers were increasing at a much greater rate. College resources were clearly seen to be most urgently needed in areas of rapid growth. At the same time, there were considerable constraints on health spending generally, with hospital beds and facilities suffering in particular. This made clinical medical teaching and research more difficult. Thus the medical faculty was caught in what could be described as a 'double whammy'.

During the 1980s, a triumvirate consisting of the president, the registrar and the finance officer/secretary seemed particularly powerful and influential in UCC. In a challenging and difficult situation, they managed the ever-growing college skilfully. They were not noted, however, for espousing with particular enthusiasm the troubles and difficulties of the medical faculty, while their relationship with an embattled Health Board was not as close as it had been over the previous twenty years (and would be again in the future). To compound the problems of the medical faculty further, it did not have a member on the governing body of the college – almost for the first time in many years – so that a valuable forum for airing its particular difficulties was not available. Lack of such representation is a surprising disadvantage.

While this author may be unwittingly exaggerating the woes of faculty at this time (morale was low), it must be stressed that not all its troubles were the faults of the national government or the college authorities. Two subjects in which the faculty must undoubtedly shoulder some of the blame were general practice and public health and hygiene/social medicine.

13

General Practice and Public Health

General Practice

The development of general practice as an academic discipline in Cork does not reflect well on UCC. During the late 1950s and early 1960s, after the College (later the Royal College) of General Practitioners had been established in Britain, an enlightened group of family doctors in the Cork area became members of that college and set out to teach general practice to undergraduates in UCC, as well as making postgraduate study and training available for the first time to young GPs. This group, who were pioneers in their efforts, included John Gowen, Ted O'Brien, Dick Cronin and Owen Shorten, to all of whom the specialty owes a great debt. A small number of lectures to undergraduates were given by them annually and, in the later 1960s and early 1970s, teaching became better organised and practical instruction in the subject began. The teaching was at first in the Department of Medicine but with the appointment of Dr (later Professor) John Corridan to social and preventive medicine, it was taken over by this department. Dr Owen K. Shorten was an enthusiastic and selfless organiser at practical level. The establishment of the Irish College of General Practitioners gave the academic status of the subject further encouragement and, in UCC, a system of student attachments to selected practices for limited periods proved both popular and productive. Dr William Shannon, who practised in the Bishopstown area close to UCC, took a deep interest in the teaching and administration of the subject and relationships between the College of General Practitioners and UCC were cordial and fruitful.

While Cork was prominent in the teaching of general practice to undergraduates, in the earlier days it was less effective when the need for an academic department in the subject headed by a professor became more obvious. In the first place, not all faculty members were convinced of this need. However, the successful developments of depart- ments elsewhere together with the advances in practice and research in the subject finally convinced the faculty and, more importantly, the college administration that Cork needed a professorial unit. Then, many difficulties in establishing it emerged. The college authorities, while in favour in principle, were slow to fund the venture and also seemed to think that it should be located in a certain practice and area of their choice. The Health Board did not agree with this, inclining rather to the view that the unit should be established in an area where they felt there was most clinical need for it. Faculty members were mainly concerned that the new chair be filled in open competition. The problems rumbled on for an unnecessarily long time with promising candidates losing patience and taking up posts elsewhere. It was not until the mid-1990s when Dr Colin P. M. Bradley, a UCD graduate of 1981 who had worked as a senior lecturer in general practice in Britain, was appointed to the new chair that the matter was resolved. This represented a satisfactory conclusion to a tediously long process.

Epidemiology and Public Health

The situation in social and community medicine/epidemiology and public health (the subject would appear to have multiple appellations), though quite different, also proved difficult to resolve. Professor Corridan retired in the late 1980s, yet the chair was not filled for a number of years. The causes for the delay were probably multiple but the main one appears to have been the reluctance of the college to meet the costs associated with

the appointment of a successor. There were, however, also difficulties about who might teach the subject and what their background should be. For a time, the subject was taught by the Director of Public Health of the Southern Health Board, Dr Elisabeth Keane and her colleagues, who kindly kept teaching going when this was very necessary. In 1997, the new professor, Dr Ivan Perry, took up duty. Since then, the subject has expanded and developed significantly and it is now a vibrant part of the medical curriculum.

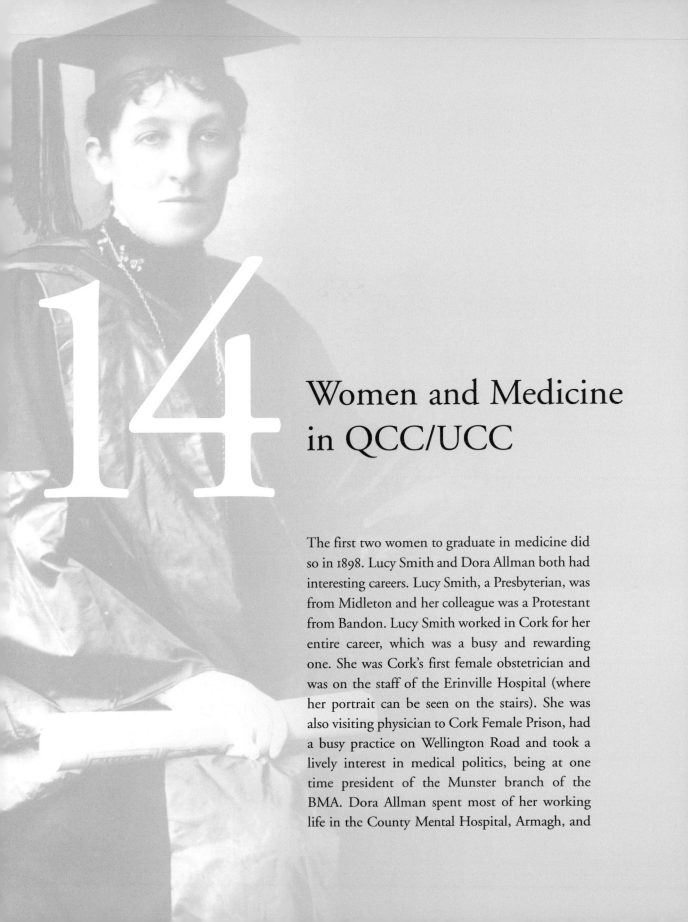

14

Women and Medicine in QCC/UCC

The first two women to graduate in medicine did so in 1898. Lucy Smith and Dora Allman both had interesting careers. Lucy Smith, a Presbyterian, was from Midleton and her colleague was a Protestant from Bandon. Lucy Smith worked in Cork for her entire career, which was a busy and rewarding one. She was Cork's first female obstetrician and was on the staff of the Erinville Hospital (where her portrait can be seen on the stairs). She was also visiting physician to Cork Female Prison, had a busy practice on Wellington Road and took a lively interest in medical politics, being at one time president of the Munster branch of the BMA. Dora Allman spent most of her working life in the County Mental Hospital, Armagh, and

Dr Lucy Smith, Cork's first female obstetrician

became its resident medical superintendent, the first woman in Ireland to attain such a post. She is still remembered in Armagh with affection and respect.

Apart from the initial pair, only a further ten women graduated in Cork during the succeeding twenty years. The next two also had un-usual careers. Jane Reynolds from Cork city graduated in 1905 and saw active service in the British armed forces for a number of years while Sarah Wolfe of the class of 1913 and from a West Cork family, spent her working life as a Wesleyan missionary in a variety of hospitals in China, at a time when life there for a European woman must have been both adventurous and hazardous.

A better known medical missionary was Anna Dengel,[1] an Austrian who received her early education in that country from the Ursuline order of nuns. She completed her second-level studies with the same order in their convent school in Blackrock in Cork. Her move to Ireland was prompted by a desire to study medicine (not feasible for a woman in Austria at the time), to learn English and to gain a British medical degree. She entered medicine at UCC in the autumn of 1914 just after the outbreak of World War I and graduated in 1919. She was strongly motivated to become a medical missionary and also a nun. At the time, the two objectives were mutually incompatible as, under Canon Law, religious sisters were precluded from working as doctors or attending childbirth. She began working in a mission hospital in Rawalpindi, India, a year after graduation and did sterling work there for more than four years, caring for

Dr Dora Allman with other staff members, County Mental Hospital, Armagh

women and children who would not otherwise have had medical care. This was because at that time women were, under the custom of purdah, prevented from seeing men, including male doctors, from outside their own families and female doctors were exceedingly scarce.

Anna Dengel went to the USA on a lecture tour in 1925 where, after much effort and a share of good fortune, she succeeded in opening the door for female doctors to a religious life, when she was given permission by the ecclesiastical authorities to establish the Society of Catholic Medical Missionaries. The sisters in this society had to be certified doctors or nurses. While the society did not receive full official approval from the Vatican until 1936, it was an immediate success and has done remarkable work through the years.

By the late 1930s, Anna Dengel's work had become internationally recognised and she was awarded many honorary doctorates and fellowships as well as awards from the Vatican and from her native Austrian government. A remarkable woman of whom the Cork medical school can be proud, she died in 1980.

By the end of World War I, significant numbers of women had begun the study of medicine and the number of women graduating was about one-quarter that of men

Anna Dengel's Honorary Conferring, 1932 (second from right, front row)

for the next forty-five years. Then the proportion began to increase markedly and this increase has continued. Now some 70 per cent of medical graduates are female.

It has long been assumed that, until recently, a sizeable proportion of women doctors did not continue to practise for longer than a few years after graduation. The diagram opposite shows that this has not been so, apart from a few years during World War II when there were very few posts in Ireland and life abroad was seen, by some, as unattractive and not very safe. While the diagram does not cover the last ten years of the twentieth century, it can be taken that virtually everyone who has graduated since 1990 has continued to practise.

While a majority of males who graduated in Cork during the first hundred years of the school ended up practising abroad, women settled in Ireland and overseas in about equal numbers. Since 1960, a small but significant majority have, like their male counterparts, worked permanently in Ireland. That female doctors have never emigrated to a greater degree is probably because of their willingness in the past to remain in Ireland in junior – or assistant – posts or alternatively in part-time employment.

Fewer women than men went into general practice, and tended to specialise in public health medicine and psychiatry. There have been an appreciable number of women

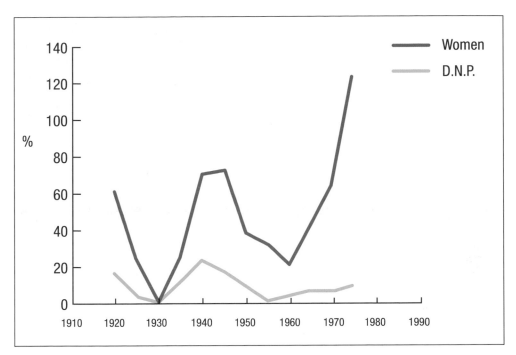

Women graduates who did and did not practise medicine

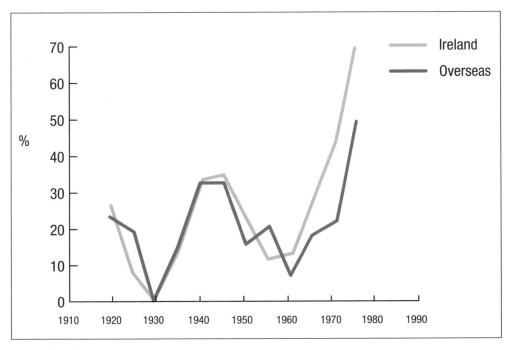

Destination of women graduates

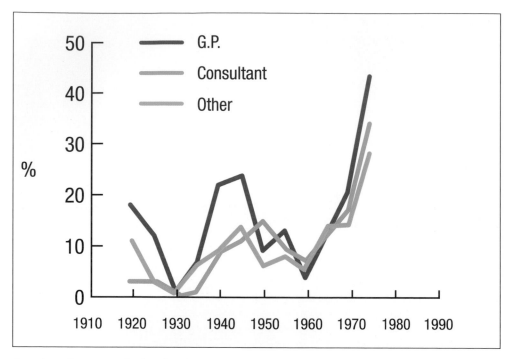

Specialties of women medical graduates

missionary doctors, like Anna Dengel and Sarah Wolfe, throughout the twentieth century. They have done, and continue to do, very valuable and quite heroic work in difficult and sometimes dangerous environments and reflect great credit on the school.

Since the middle of the 1970s, the situation of women in medicine at UCC has changed greatly. There are now more female students and graduates than there are male. The change has been too recent for its impact to be fully assessed and, furthermore, the process appears to be ongoing. There can, however, be no doubt of its significance – social, medical and economic. It is of course not confined to Cork, or indeed to Ireland, and its implications are almost certainly under active consideration by doctors, administrators and planners.

The increase in the numbers of women graduates has not so far been accompanied by a comparable increase in women teachers in medicine, particularly at senior levels. Here, it is still very much a man's world and none of the clinical or pre-clinical departments have had women as heads; indeed there have been few enough of them in teaching posts at any level. While reasons can be found up to the present for the striking disparity between the numbers of women students and teachers, it will be very interesting to see if it continues into a future which will be numerically dominated by female doctors.

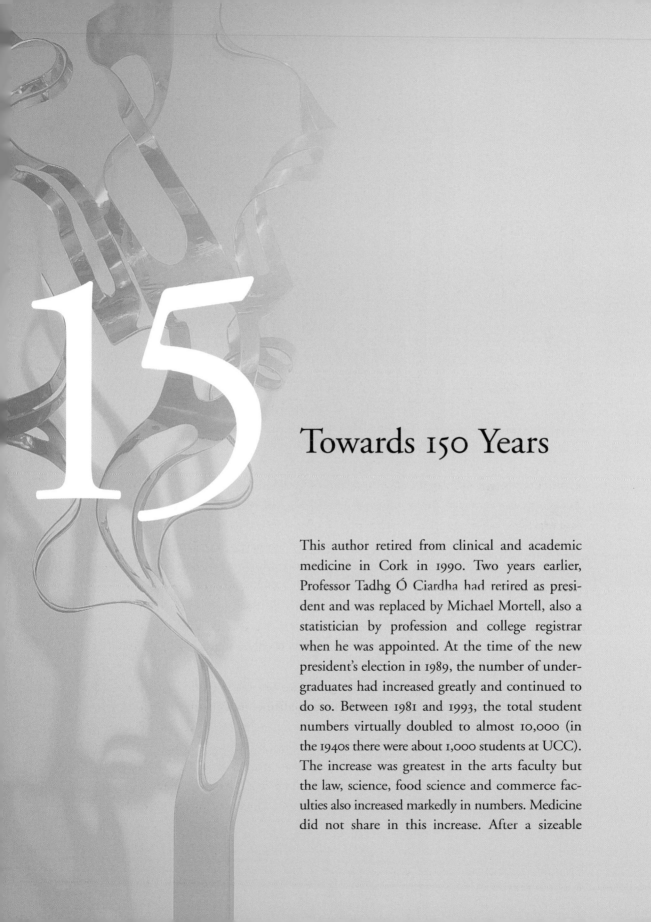

15

Towards 150 Years

This author retired from clinical and academic medicine in Cork in 1990. Two years earlier, Professor Tadhg Ó Ciardha had retired as president and was replaced by Michael Mortell, also a statistician by profession and college registrar when he was appointed. At the time of the new president's election in 1989, the number of undergraduates had increased greatly and continued to do so. Between 1981 and 1993, the total student numbers virtually doubled to almost 10,000 (in the 1940s there were about 1,000 students at UCC). The increase was greatest in the arts faculty but the law, science, food science and commerce faculties also increased markedly in numbers. Medicine did not share in this increase. After a sizeable

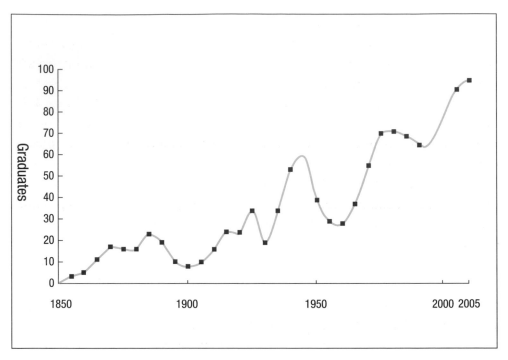

Medical graduate numbers, 1850–2005

expansion in the late 1960s and early 1970s, student numbers remained virtually unchanged for the next two decades. This, as has been explained, was not due to lack of demand for places – on the contrary, entry to medicine was the most sought after of all the faculties – but by the consistent limitation imposed by central authorities on the number of Irish (and later EU) nationals allowed to graduate.

The gross and increasing disparity between the burgeoning numbers in the college generally and the static situation (apart from the increase in non-EU students) in medicine, did not have a good effect on the morale or on the economic health of the medical faculty. An increasing demand for the development and extension of postgraduate medical education and research could certainly not be financed from central funding and while the substantial fees paid by the now increasing number of non-EU medical students were of some help to the college generally, they were not going to be of great significance in relieving medical needs.

Some economic help and a much-needed boost to the medical school's morale was provided by the medical graduates themselves. Since the 1970s, medical alumni have been meeting annually at UCC in an informal fashion at a postgraduate medical seminar which combined scientific lectures with social events. This humble beginning became the basis for the foundation of a Medical Graduates Association in the late 1980s and early 1990s, whose aims were to provide scientific, educational and social opportunities for Cork medical alumni and to help the development of the school by giving it financial assistance. In its early years particularly, it received considerable support from Cork medical graduates – both Irish and American-born – who were working in the USA and Canada. Sizeable sums of money were raised, both at home and abroad, at a time when funding was desperately needed for postgraduate education. Of equal importance was that it provided a means of keeping graduates in touch with the college and with each other and it has been the fulcrum around which many class reunions and similar events have been built. It continues to thrive, and among its other activities publishes a news journal twice-yearly which is both appreciated by the alumni and of value to the medical school.

During the early 1990s, two very important appointments were made in the medical faculty when the chair of clinical pharmacology was established and filled, and a new Professor of Medicine took office. The first Professor of Clinical Pharmacology/ Therapeutics, Dr Michael B. Murphy, a UCC graduate of 1976, trained in London and Chicago where his main research interests were in the management of hypertension. On his return to Cork, he worked at the Mercy Hospital and the Cork University Hospital, soon building a strong unit and attracting significant support for his research projects, which are widely acknowledged. He became Dean of Medicine in 2000 and has been a central figure in the development and expansion of the faculty, which is out-lined in the following chapter.

The chair of medicine remained unfilled for three years until 1993, when Dr Fergus Shanahan, a UCD graduate of 1977, became professor. Much of his postgraduate training was at McMaster University in Canada and later at the University College of Los Angeles (UCLA) in California. A consultant gastroenterologist whose specialty is inflammatory bowel disease, he has developed a department of international repute and, by close co-operation with other units such as food science and with other hospitals (notably the Mercy Hospital), he has built an innovative and highly productive research team.

As these two recent appointees were finding their feet, the Irish economy began to improve dramatically and the Celtic Tiger was on its way. It could not have come at a more opportune time for a medical faculty which was eager and able to benefit from it. As the college was celebrating the 150th anniversary of its incorporation, one of its three original faculties was poised to enter a new era.

It will be remembered that Queen Victoria, after whom the original Queen's College was named, paid her first visit to the city in August 1849 as the building of her college

Statue of Queen Victoria, Staff Common Room, UCC

was almost complete. A statue in her honour was erected as she passed by along the Western Road, and it remained in the main tower of the college for nearly a century. In the 1930s, however, nationalism was strong in UCC and there was a general feeling that the statue was inappropriate in its very prominent position and should be removed. This was done in 1934 when it was taken down and replaced by a statue of St Finbarr, the patron saint of the diocese and of the college, sculpted by the then youthful Seamus Murphy. Victoria was placed in an office in the East Wing of the main college building where, in time, it proved too heavy for the floorboards. Accordingly, it was removed and, without ceremony and certainly without publicity, buried in the president's garden. It lay there unmarked and largely forgotten until preparations for the 150th anniversary were being finalised. Then she was exhumed (not without some mild protests) and displayed in the old council room. The statue remains on exhibition there and is much admired – it is one of the few statues of the young queen. It is tempting to ponder on what she might think of her Cork college were she to revisit it.

16 Ten Years On, 2005

The purpose of this book is to tell the story of the Cork medical school during its first 150 years (1845–1995). Writing ten years later, it seems unrealistic not to at least mention the striking changes that have taken place in the intervening decade. This writer is ill-equipped to do this, so in writing the present chapter has relied on information supplied by the medical faculty, particularly professors Michael Murphy and Eamonn Quigley, to whom he is deeply indebted.

In 1995, there were 540 medical and 140 dental undergraduates who with between ten and fifteen postgraduates brought the total student population to almost 700. Since then, the faculty has changed not only in name but also encompasses a much

Brookfield Health Sciences Complex

wider range of disciplines. A School of Nursing and Midwifery was instituted in 1994, a School of Pharmacy in 2002 and a School of Clinical Therapies (encompassing occupational therapy and the Department of Speech and Hearing Sciences) in 2003. The new faculty, now entitled the Faculty of Medicine and Health, comprises 2,600 students of which 630 are medical undergraduates and 100 public health students. There are 309 full-time staff and 420 part-time/ad hoc teachers. The dean, Professor Michael Murphy, formerly regarded as simply the Dean of Medicine, became the Dean of Medicine and Health, while responsibility for the day-to-day running of the medical school fell to the newly created Head of School, Professor Eamonn Quigley.

Many capital projects have taken place. The most notable of these is the Brookfield Health Sciences Complex catering for medicine, nursing and the clinical therapies. The complex is situated on College Road and is accommodated in a striking building which encompasses and surrounds the house once occupied by the Jennings family. The nursing section has been in use for over a year and the medicine and therapies units were officially opened on 28 November 2005. The move has been timely and will, for the first time in history, provide the school with dedicated teaching and administrative space including clinical and communications skills laboratories. The School of Pharmacy, on a separate site on College Road, opened in March 2006. The two units comprising obstetrics clinical research and teaching, situated with the Cork University Maternity Hospital in front of the Cork University Hospital, will open in 2007. The hospital will replace the Erinville, St Finbarr's and the Bon Secours Maternity Units with more than 7,000 deliveries a year. The cost is over €80 million, and there is a planned staff of seventeen consultant obstetricians. It is by far the largest clinical maternity unit ever developed in Munster and its potential for obstetrics and gynaecology as well as for neonatology is immense.

There have also been significant developments in academic appointments in the medical school. Chairs have been established in anaesthetics, radiology and medical imaging, medical microbiology, cellular physiology and cardiovascular science and there has been a burgeoning number of appointments at professorial, senior lecturer and consultant levels in already established academic disciplines.

The financial costs of the projects described are clearly very large, impossibly so in the perceptions of older, and even not so old, graduates. In the early 1990s, President Michael Mortell recognised the potential of acquiring serious funding for research and other projects from former graduates both at home and abroad and vigorously promoted alumni associations worldwide. While monies so acquired were appreciable, they were in great demand in a rapidly expanding and underfunded college. Medical alumni tried to go it alone and were generous in their giving but amounts received were far from adequate for the development and research needs of the faculty. Separate phenomena in the later 1990s combined, however, to make research funds available. The first of these was that a number of the newer, senior appointees to medical faculty were skilled research workers who had both the ability and energy to conceive and organise promising research projects which found favour with those who would be in a position to fund them. The second was the advent of the Celtic Tiger, together with the realisation by those in authority that high-class, scientific research projects in third-level institutions were valuable instruments in fuelling the economic boom. A further very important factor was the appointment of Professor G. T. Wrixon as president in 1999. He, perhaps more than any of his predecessors, realised the value and critical importance of promoting research and gaining funds to do so. His own record in both these regards was impeccable and he gave invaluable support to individual departments in the faculty.

From these beginnings, the Cork medical school has become a major force in biomedical research on the international stage and research, both basic and clinical, is a fundamental component of every discipline in faculty. Fruitful collaborations have

Medical graduates, 1962 (the author, Denis O'Sullivan, is third from right, front row)

Medical graduates, 2006

developed across departments and faculties as well as with institutions and individuals both in Ireland and abroad. An example of the new climate of research in UCC is the Alimentary Pharmabiotic Centre which was established through the largest grant ever bestowed on an institution in the biomedical area in Ireland by Science Foundation Ireland. The centre, under the direction of Fergus Shanahan, combines clinicians from a number of medical faculty specialties, such as medicine and psychiatry, with scientists from microbiology, molecular biology and immunology, not only in UCC but from Teagasc, at Moorepark, to tackle the complexities of the interactions between the hosts and the enteric flora. Collaborations with industry as well as with academic colleagues worldwide have been built up in a variety of disciplines and, in this way, Cork can and does compete at the very highest level. Research is emphasised at all stages and students as well as graduates are encouraged to participate from the very beginning of their studies.

A number of other improvements, both structural and academic have taken place over the past ten years, with more in various stages of completion or planning. An increase in student numbers is contemplated including a graduate entry stream. Further development of research and postgraduate opportunities is high on the faculty's agenda. There is a vibrant atmosphere throughout the school with confidence for the future evident at every level. Hopefully, the core values which have characterised Cork throughout the years are being retained; a sound basis in science, a realisation of the paramount importance of good clinical teaching and a constant reminder that the school must continue to serve the people of Munster by improving their health and ensuring optimal standards of diagnosis and treatment of disease.

Pictures can often tell tales more effectively than the written word, so this chapter concludes with the graduation photograph of the class of 1962 (this author's first year on the staff of UCC) and that of the most recent graduates, the class of 2006.

Brookfield Health Sciences Complex, UCC

Epilogue

The Cork medical school has prospered and is held in high regard in Ireland and internationally. Much of the credit for this is due to the present faculty and to the college president and administration who have been creative, hardworking and perceptive. In acknowledging their efforts and successes, it is also important to look back at the school over the years with its many ups and downs, triumphs and failures. Only one aspect of the school seems to have been consistently satisfactory – the quality of its graduates. This has been acknowledged and commented on wherever they worked. Why it should be so has been questioned in the past; Blennerhasset, president at the end of the nineteenth century, attributed it to the fact that the people of south Munster were intellectually talented beyond the norm but, like many of his other views, this can hardly be taken seriously! It would seem much more likely that Cork produced good doctors because they were well taught, often by teachers who were overworked and underpaid but persistently dedicated to what they perceived as their obligation to obey the strictures of the Hippocratic Oath.

Most of the major changes in the medical school have taken place over the past fifty years. The most striking of these have probably happened during the past fifteen but since the visitations during the middle 1950s and early 1960s, the medical faculty has been striving mightily to achieve a school of high quality which compares favourably with the best in these islands and elsewhere. That it has succeeded in so doing is attributable in considerable part to the tireless and unstinting efforts of its members over this time. Happily, many of these have lived to witness the results of their labours. Hopefully, their efforts will be appreciated by those who now and in future years benefit from them.

The success of any school has to be judged by its end product; the graduates. Cork graduates through the years have, as we have seen, done their alma mater proud and continue to do so. It is to them that this book is dedicated, with affection and pride.

Notes

Chapter 1

1. Murphy, John A., *The College* (Cork, 1995) p. 30.
2. Coakley, Davis, Personal Letter (1999).
3. *The Medical Directory*, The Cork School of Medicine (London, 1861) p. 960.
4. The Anatomy Act, 2 & 3, William IV Chapter 75 (1832) pp. 1–4.
5. Murphy, *The College*, p. 96.

Chapter 2

1. Cameron C. A., *History of the Royal College of Surgeons in Ireland and of the Irish Schools of Medicine* 2nd Edition (Dublin, 1916) p. 681.
2. Kane, R., Chief Secretary's Official Regional Papers (1849) 01007.
3. Murphy, *The College*, p. 81.
4. O'Rahilly, R., *A History of the Cork School of Medicine, 1849–1949* (Cork, 1949) p. 15.

Chapter 3

1. O'Rahilly, *A History of the Cork School of Medicine, 1849–1949*, p. 25.
2. Murphy, *The College*, p. 161.
3. *Ibid*, p. 129.

Chapter 4

1. Pearson, C. Y., *Quarryman* (March 1931) p. 43.
2. O'Rahilly, *A History of the Cork School of Medicine, 1849–1949*, pp. 27-30.
3. British Medical Association, *British Medical Journal*, vol 2 (London, 1879).
4. British Medical Association, *British Medical Journal*, vol 2 (London, 1923) p. 788. See also, O'Rahilly, *A History of the Cork School of Medicine, 1849–1949*, p 48.

Chapter 5

1. Taylor M., *Sir Bertram Windle: A Memoir* (London, 1932) p. 386.

Chapter 6

1. Murphy, *The College*, p. 206.

Chapter 7

1. O'Rahilly, A., 'The proposed full-time state official for obstetrics and gynaecology', *Cork University Record* (1952).
2. O'Donovan, J. M., 'Address at the conferring of degrees', *Cork University Record* (1952).
3. Council on medical education and hospitals, *American Medical Association Visitation Report* (UCC Archives, uc/po/320) (1953) pp. 1–5.
4. General Medical Council, *Visitors' Report* (UCC archives uc/po/320) (London, 1954) pp. 1-20.
5. *Ibid.*, p. 7.
6. O'Rahilly A., 'The Cork Medical School', *Cork University Record* (1954).
7. Atkins, H. St J., 'Address at the conferring of degrees', *Cork University Record* (1954).
8. Gordon, Robert, *Doctor at Large* (London, 1955).

Chapter 8

1. *Report on joint visitation of medical schools in the Republic of Ireland,* Medical Registration Council of Ireland, pp. 1–24.
2. O'Sullivan, S., 'Cork Regional Hospital Saga', *Evening Echo* (1 September 1972).

Chapter 9

1. Cockburn P., *The Broken Boy* (London, 2005) p. 34.
2. Murphy, *The College*, pp. 311–312.

Chapter 10

1. Conlon, M. V., *Journal of the Cork Historical and Archaeological Society* (Cork, 1943) p. 76.
2. Cummins N. Marshall, *Some Chapters of Cork History* (Cork, 1957) Chapter 1, p. 1.

Chapter 11

1. Cummins, *Some Chapters of Cork History*, Chapter 5, p. 27.
2. Henry H. M., *Our Lady's Psychiatric Hospital* (Cork, 1989) p. 69.

Chapter 14

1. Medical Mission Sisters Editorial Board, *Fire and Flame: The Legacy of Anna Dengel* (Philadelphia, 1998) pp. 1–24.

Index

O'Sullivan, W. M., *45*
Our Lady's Hospital (Cork Mental Hospital), 44, 68, 90
    see also Eglinton Asylum

P
Pearson, Charles Yelverton, 26, 31–2, 41, 44
    Modern Surgical Technique, 32
Perry, Ivan, 98
Presbyterians, 19
public health *see* epidemiology

Q
Quakers, 19
Quarry, Revd Dr, 82
Queen's College Belfast, 1, 37
Queen's College Cork *see* University College Cork
Queen's College Galway, 1, 27, 37
Quigley, Eamonn, 109, 110

R
Recognised School of Medicine, 4
Redmond, John, 37
research and funding, 45, 66, 106, 111–13
Reynolds, Jane, 100
Rosscarbery, West Cork, 43
Royal College of Physicians of Ireland, 3
Royal College of General Practioners, 95
Royal University of Ireland, 17, 27, 30
rugby football, 45–6
Russell, Jack, *45*, 46
Ryall, John, 1

S
St Finbarr's Hospital (Cork District Hospital), 31, 55, 57,
    58, 59, 60, 61, 63, 64, 65–6, 68, 69, 76, 77, 78, 79,
    86–9, 111
        pathology department, 67–8
St Finbarr's Seminary, 26
St Mary's Church, Pope's Quay, 2
St Mary's Orthopaedic Hospital, 67
St Patrick's Hospital, 43
St Stephen's Hospital, 61, 67, 90
    psychiatry department, 68
Sandford, Arthur W., 44, 85
School of Anatomy, 4

School of Anatomy, Medicine and Surgery, 4
School of Pharmacy, 111
Science Foundation Ireland, 113
Shanahan, Fergus, 107, 113
Shannon, William, 96
Sheehan, John D., 70, 74
Shorten, Owen K., 66, 95, 96
Sigerson, George, 46
Sisters of Mercy, 80
Slattery, James W., 30
Smith, Lucy, 99
Society of Catholic Medical Missionaries, 101
Society of St Vincent de Paul, 48
South Infirmary, 3, 4, 26, 43, 51, 53, 79, 80–2, 86
    amalgamated with Victoria Hospital (1988), 82
    see also Victoria Hospital
Stokes, William, 5
Sullivan, William Kirby, 12, 27–9, 90
Sutton, Reginald C., 86

T
Teagasc, 113
Teehan, Charlie, 46
Thecla, Sr. M., *77*
Toronto University, 38
Townsend, Edward Richard, 31
Trinity College Dublin, 4, 8, 18, 22, 35, 37

U
ultramontanism, 14
United Irishmen, 4
University College Cork (Queen's College Cork), 4, 6,
    13, 93, 95, 96
    Aula Maxima, 2, 29
    BMA meeting, 27–9
    career choices of students, 20–4, 56
    Church opposition to, 14, 18–19, 33, 37, 40
    election procedures, 40–1
    fire (1862), 12–14, 27
    non-EU students, 92–3, 93, 106
    opening of, 2–3, 15
    social background of students, 19–20
    social life of students, 45–8
    student numbers, 15–17, 30, 39–40, 45, 50, 53,
        55–6, 66, 70–1, 75, 92, 93, 105–6, 109